AN INTRODUCTION TO
THE SOCIOLOGY OF THE NEW TESTAMENT

AN INTRODUCTION TO THE

SOCIOLOGY

OF THE

NEW TESTAMENT

DEREK TIDBALL

Exeter
The Paternoster Press

AUSTRALIA:
Bookhouse Australia
P.O. Box 115, Flemington Markets, NSW 2129

SOUTH AFRICA:
Oxford University Press, P.O. Box 1141, Cape Town

British Library Cataloguing in Publication Data
Tidball, Derek
    An Introduction to the Sociology of the New Testament:
    1. Bible. N. T. — Criticism, Interpretation, etc.
    I. Title
    225.6 BS2361.2

ISBN 0-85364-301-6

Set in 11pt Plantin by Nuprint Services Ltd, Harpenden, Herts and printed
by A. Wheaton & Co. Ltd., Exeter, for THE PATERNOSTER PRESS LTD,
Paternoster House, 3 Mount Radford Crescent, Exeter, Devon

To
Joan and Ken Tidball

Contents

Introduction

The application of a sociological perspective to the new Testament is not a new idea but it is currently undergoing something of a revival. It seems destined to be more than a passing fashion and to hold promise as a means by which we can understand parts of the New Testament with greater clarity. Not all recent writing in this area has been illuminating, some has been fanciful, but much has been worthwhile and fruitful.

It is the intention of this book to introduce the reader to some of the current discussion in this area and to provide a guide to the literature available. Some of the most stimulating material is buried in the more inaccessible academic journals and so not easily available except to those well motivated to pursue their quest. But it is a pity that articles that can help our understanding should enjoy such limited circulation.

This book has been written for the general reader rather than the specialist. The author has therefore tried to avoid using much of the complex jargon that so bedevils sociology. His friends and students will doubtless tell him in due course how successful he has been in fulfilling this aim. It is hoped, however, that the book will provide a straightforward introduction which will inform and stimulate and bring better understanding of the New Testament itself. Consistent with its purpose, there is no attempt to be original although a critical assessment of current thinking is made from the standpoint of one who is committed to a conservative view of the New Testament. Furthermore some liberty has been taken on occasions to apply the discoveries to the contemporary church.

Before reviewing the New Testament itself Chapter 1 assesses the difficulties inherent in the task and discusses the often troubled relationship between sociology and faith. It is made abundantly clear in that chapter that any conclusions reached must be tentative and modest—not least because the evidence on which one builds is so often slender. There is therefore little room for dogmatism and much room for humility. If however one succeeds in reinstating the New Testament church as a body of ordinary people with down-to-earth flesh and blood concerns and delivers them from the assumption so often made that they must have all been budding academic theologians the task, however limited, will have been worthwhile.

Since originally writing this manuscript a number of important works have been published which have extended the discussion. For the most part it has been possible to allude to these in the footnotes. Howard Kee, to whom reference is made in Chapter 2, has once more contributed to the discussion by the publication of *Christian Origins in Sociological Perspective* (S.C.M., 1980). Although much of the ground covered is similar, incorporating references to it into the present text would not have done justice to the different perspective Kee presents. Since it merited more extensive engagement than was possible at the present time it was thought best to omit reference to it altogether.

The most recent publication in the field extends the subject even further. Bruce J. Malina's *The New Testament World* (S.C.M., 1983) provides, as its sub-title suggests, insights from cultural anthropology. Approaching the New Testament from the related discipline of anthropology rather than sociology it takes the value of honour as its starting point and traces its outworking in New Testament culture in relation to personality, possessions, kinship and purity. The work is very readable and should prove an excellent stimulus for those who want to understand the New Testament.

I am grateful to many for their assistance in one form or another in the writing of this book. In particular, mention should be made of Clifford Hill who wrote his docotoral thesis for the University of Nottingham on this topic in 1972. It was the reading of that thesis some years ago that stimulated my own interest in this area and I am grateful to him for his permission to refer to his work in the following pages. The opinions of the present book however are attributable to me.

Among others to whom I would like to pay tribute are my parents. This work is dedicated to them for their support and encouragement through the years in which I have been studying. Without them, for more than the obvious reasons, I would not have been able to have the pleasure of working at the New Testament nor of believing in the relevance of its message.

DEREK J. TIDBALL

CHAPTER ONE

Problems and Perspective

The ordinary believer might view the advances of sociology
into the field of the New Testament as a matter of imper-
tinence if not of profound disquiet. He may well feel that he
faces enough problems in the interpretation and application of
his faith as it is. The amorous overtures of the boom industry
of sociology, he suspects, will not only complicate his problems but even undermine the conclusions he has already
reached.

Theologians have not, as a whole, greeted the intrusion of
sociology any more warmly. Despite a number of venerable
attempts to use a sociological perspective to illuminate the
New Testament[1] theologians have largely remained content to
continue using their own well-worn tools and methods. In fair-
ness there has recently been a new emphasis on the setting in
which the various parts of the New Testament writings were
written and the purpose which lay behind them. But theologians have usually been happy to discover academic issues
lying behind the writings; reflecting, one suspects, more the
interests of the theologians themselves than the real interests
of the first century writers. This has given, as Howard Kee
suggests, the impression that 'theological affirmations were
formed during the early decades of the Church's existence by a
process of intellectual debate—the first century equivalent of
a present day theological seminar'.[2]

It is true that sociology can be a disturbing discipline. Peter
Berger, has admitted that it 'is not conducive to an onward—
and—upward outlook, but will rather lead to one degree or
another of disenchantment with regard to the interpretations
of social reality given in Sunday Schools . . .,[3] or, one might
add even in theological colleges. Nonetheless it is also a fruit-

ful and illuminating discipline. Above all it tries to keep real flesh and blood human beings at the forefront of the stage in all the complexity of their social relationships and turmoil of their social situations. So it makes it more difficult either to idealise what we read of the early disciples or to over-theorise about them. And we stand to gain fresh insights into the understanding of the New Testament.

Such a task however needs to be handled with care. It is well to face the problems and perspectives honestly before we begin.

SOCIOLOGY AND ITS PERSPECTIVE

Defining sociology is no easy task. There are almost as many definitions of sociology as there are sociologists. However else one might define it, sociology is certainly an attempt to understand society and social relations within society in a disciplined way. To the layman the understanding of society may seem straightforward. From experience however a sociologist has learned that the obvious is not always quite so obvious as it seems. So when he describes a social relationship he has probed beneath the surface to gain a real understanding of what was involved in the social behaviour he is considering.

In order to gain this understanding he will use various tools and methods which can be tested and validated by others. Part of the richness and diversity of the discipline lies in the fact that different methods have been developed independently of each other. So there sometimes appears to be little coherence between the pronouncements of one sociologist and those of another.

Among the range of interests covered by sociologists various recurring themes stand out. Bare description of a man in his relationships with other men is not usually sufficient to excite the interest of a sociologist—even though that in itself might be a difficult task. Relationships are not static; they change and develop. So a sociologist is concerned at what makes for change and what inhibits change. If the sociologist is painting on a large canvas this develops into social history. And in order to write sociology on that scale he will need some framework in which to understand man's social organisation; the social forces man creates and those which shape him; the network of social classes involved; his ideas of authority and community and so on.

Clearly such a task is bound to involve the sociologist in

interpreting what he sees. No description of social reality can be exempt from such interpretation but one must always strive to make the interpretation fit the reality and not the reality fit the interpretation. The analytic methods and concepts of the sociologist must always remain his tools not become his master.

More recently sociologists have delved even more deeply into man's social life. From the time a baby is born he begins to see the world in which he lives in a certain kind of way. It is not merely that he is socialised into certain roles, e.g., the role of a boy or a girl; a pupil, a football fan or what have you. It is deeper and more fundamental than that. He receives an interpretation of the world which becomes such a part of him that he believes his interpretation to be none other than reality itself. For example, a child in England will assume that the only way for human beings to communicate with each other is by the English language. And he will initially have difficulty in understanding why and how others speak French, German or Urdu. To him English is 'real' and other languages are not. Most of us eventually overcome this difficulty but even so a good many adults continue to experience frustration when on their packaged holidays they discover that 'foreigners' don't speak English as they might be expected to!

What applies to our language applies to our whole experience. We live every day in the light of a picture of the world we have received and which we do not often question because we believe it to be real. Most of the time we are not even conscious of it. This is not to say that we are totally passive recipients of this world view. As time passes the view we have received of the world changes. Sometimes we challenge it and help to change it. We both partly create it and are partly created by it.

Sociologists then look at what men believe and how men interpret the world in which they live from where they stand i.e., in relation to the social context in which they live. They speak of this as man's social construction of reality.[4] Since no field of man's knowledge is exempt from their scrutiny, mathematics, language and ordinary everyday affairs are investigated in this way. Religion is also seen in this light. Every man experiences certain things at the margins of his life which do not make sense, like dreams or death, or things which go beyond normal explanations and excite wonder and awe such as the birth of a child. In order to help him cope with these and many other uncertain experiences he interprets reality in a certain way. He gives a sacred interpretation to it.

In so doing he overcomes some of the uncertainties and finds significance as a man. It is an interpretation that overarches all his other interpretations in life as an umbrella covers a man. Man's interpretation of life may or may not correspond to the existence of an objective reality. In the case of a religious interpretation the reality which may or may not exist is God. In any case the understanding of this reality is always socially constructed. And because it is always socially constructed it is never absolutely sure; it is always precarious. The most threatening position of all is when few other people share your interpretation of reality and it becomes less and less plausible for you to believe in it. Sociologists use this process to describe the present difficulties of many believers in the twentieth century. They are a small minority surrounded by a great secular sea and therefore many find it difficult to go on believing. Reality is largely interpreted in other terms, secular or scientific terms, and these rather than the religious ones seem plausible.

The perspective of sociology clearly has considerable implications for the Christian believer which need careful attention. But before examining the problems that exist in the relationship between sociology and the New Testament it would be helpful to summarise what the discipline of sociology can offer to an understanding of the New Testament.

Jonathan Smith, in an influential paper delivered in Chicago in 1973[5] outlined four areas in which sociology illuminates the New Testament. Firstly, it can describe the social facts of early Christianity and place it in its social context. Secondly, it can construct a social history of Christianity. Thirdly it can examine the social forces which led to Christianity and the social institutions which resulted from its foundation. Fourthly it can investigate the creation of the Christian's world view, his social construction of reality and the structures which maintained that world view as plausible.

The contribution, then, that sociology can make to our understanding of the New Testament is quite significant. It will help us to understand the growth and development of Christianity as a social movement bearing in mind as we do so the types of authority it demonstrated; the social classes it attracted; the social structure which crystalised and the social effects it had. As Clifford Hill has pointed out, this will not simply add another dimension to our knowledge, it will help us to see the whole picture in a new light.[6] We shall move from a two-dimensional to a three dimensional perspective.

Clifford Hill is right in his mild protest that 'members of the primitive church were not *only* the products of a theological ideal' but also the product of their social context.[7] The church which arose was not just a theological idea. Christians are used to viewing the Church in a number of theological ways such as the body of Christ or the bride of Christ. Yet it was and is right in addition to view it as a social institution which grew and exists in an actual and concrete world. If we fail to take this seriously we must inevitably fail to understand fully the behaviour of the church's members. Fuller understanding of the whole of the New Testament will come if we are able to see it in a sociological perspective.

Such a position is no more than the New Testament itself expects. God, though transcendent, is not totally removed from his world. The very basis of the doctrine of the Incarnation is that God became a man in Jesus of Nazareth and lived on earth as a human being. The humanness of his life did not contradict the power of God, it rather enchanced it. Similarly, the apostle Paul is aware that God chooses to use very fallible human beings, 'earthern vessels' as he calls them, to achieve his will. It is not only human beings who are fallible; it is also social groups and the structures of society. Even so, God is great enough not to ignore or override them but to use them for his own purposes 'to show that the transcendent power belongs to God and not to us'.[8]

THEOLOGICAL PROBLEMS WITH SOCIOLOGY

Enough has been said already to cause a Christian believer some fears about the explanation that sociology might give of his faith or of the New Testament. Berger has been quoted as saying that sociology often results in a modification of the views one received in Sunday School. It has been admitted that sociology involves the interpretation of social behaviour and it is well known that some of the interpretations which have been offered of religious behaviour have hardly given the believer grounds for confidence in his faith. The early history of sociology was shaped by those who thought that religion was an illusion out of which man would one day grow. It is also well-known that Durkheim[9], who was one of the few early sociologists to treat religion as the worship of something *real*, concluded that what man was doing when he was engaged in worship was recreating the soul of his own society. So even he left no room for a personal and transcendent God.

To these difficulties must be added that of relating the

sociological view of knowledge to the sort of sureness of belief which Christians experience. If what we know and if how we interpret the world really is socially determined how can we be so sure that we have the truth? The confidence expressed by the apostle John in his first epistle[10] becomes an anachronism and all belief becomes relative. If this perspective is right it must be remembered that it is not only religion and ideological belief which becomes relative but the whole of science, the pronouncements of psychology and even the musings of sociology itself. So it either leads to complete agnosticism or we must believe that even if reality is socially constructed it is possible to distinguish in other ways between valid and invalid social constructions.

It must be admitted that Christianity and sociology do sometimes appear to be contradicting each other and these contradictions must be honestly faced. Even so the Christian need not be intimidated by the findings of the sociologist concerning either his own faith or be negative and fearful in his attitude towards sociology if he bears a number of points in mind.

The proper subject matter of sociology is man in his social relationships. Since part of man's social relationships may well be religious in character, religious behaviour is a proper subject for the investigation of a sociologist. God, though active in our world and through his people, is not a man and therefore not an easy reality for sociologists to investigate.

Does that imply that sociologists are necessarily atheists; men who have to exclude the possibility that there is a God? No, it does not. Two other implications should be drawn instead.

Firstly the aim of the sociologist is to attempt to understand man's behaviour. He cannot do this by standing at a distance with his presuppositions already formed and by making superficial pronouncements on a given piece of behaviour. To be sure he has to aim for objectivity. But if he is to *understand* social behaviour he also has to try to put himself in the place of the person who is engaged in it. Really to understand religious behaviour therefore he must approach it 'as if' it were true. Only so will he learn what it means to be a believer.

Secondly it is important to remember that it is not the concern of sociology to judge whether any particular belief or behaviour is right or wrong; valid or invalid; truth or falsehood. He can describe social origin and social effect. He can say whether, according to his own declared standards, such belief or behaviour is beneficial or not for other men. But such value judgments are not within the scope of his discipline. For example, sociologists may say that the sociological origin of a sect of believers in flying-saucers from Mars is to be found in the particular place the believers have in the social structure of their society. They may explain that other members of that society are not believers in the flying saucers because they do not have the need to compensate for their social situation in the same way as believers do. But to argue like this is to leave to one side whether there are any flying saucers coming from Mars and whether their belief corresponds to an actual reality or not! The validity of their belief has to be tested in other ways.

The root of the tensions which exist between a sociological interpretation of behaviour and a theological interpretation of the same behaviour usually lies in the imperialist claims which each discipline makes. That is a sociologist is being imperial when he claims that his explanation of behaviour is the total explanation of that behaviour. Or to put it another way, he is a reductionist in that he says that his version of reality is the only valid explanation and ultimately all explanations are reduced or boil down to nothing but his own. Similarly Christians may claim that the problems in society are caused by sin and that is all there is to it. Such a claim, however, would be equally imperialist or reductionist.

Reality is more complex than this and precisely because of its intricate and wonderful complexity multiple explanations are necessary and possible. It is true, for example, that all the problems in society are caused by sin—man's failure to live as God had declared he should. It can also be true, without any contradiction whatsoever, to say they are the result of inadequate diets, or insufficient education, etc. These explanations are complementary and not contradictory.

Sociologists often present their subject in a reductionist way; but to do so is not valid. It may well be true that a movement arises because of a new formation of social classes within a society at a given time. But it may be equally legitimate to explain the rise of the movement in other terms, e.g., psychologically or theologically, without any sense of contradiction. Sociology therefore does not so much give the explanation of man's behaviour as a legitimate explanation from one viewpoint. To take one pertinent example: the growth of the early church is explained in Acts 2:47, 4:31 and 9:31 as due to the activity of the Holy Spirit. Without any lessening of belief in the Holy Spirit a Christian may also believe from a sociological perspective that the growth was due to the particular social forces at work within Judea at the time. If, as Christians believe, God is both creator and sovereign in his world it would seem quite in order that he should use normal sociological channels to accomplish his will. It would also be no matter of surprise at all if he chose to work in a different way from that which sociologists expect and so occasionally make it difficult for them to come up with a satisfactory sociological explanation of behaviour.

There is no need for the Christian to feel driven back further and further in the light of the advances of sociology until all his cherished beliefs have been explained away except for a very small 'gap' which he still explains by reference to God. Rather he is to recognise that the same behaviour can be viewed from different viewpoints and the perspectives can be complementary.[11]

We are however still left with the problem as to what we can do when sociology and theology appear to be in conflict and when they cannot be faulted on their own terms. Traditionally a number of answers have been suggested and although they do not readily resolve the conflicts they do enable us to approach them with less apprehension. All scholarship is tentative and the findings of yesterday are often revised if not rejected today. So at the point of conflict we might argue that further research is needed and that more information would lead to a resolution of the conflict. Alternatively we might argue that one or other of the disciplines is wrong and needs re-interpreting in the light of information gained by the other discipline. A classic example of the need for the teaching of the church to be re-interpreted in this respect is to be found in the case of Galileo who supported the Copernican theory that the universe revolved around the sun rather than, as traditionally taught, around the earth. We now see that it was foolish for the church to maintain steadfastly its mis-interpretation of Scripture in the light of Galileo's astronomic discoveries.

So today both the discipline of theology and sociology need to be open to each other's findings, but to be open in a discerning way. Only so can both disciplines develop in a healthy way. It is for this reason that in the work which follows the suggestions of sociologists as to how the New Testament is to be interpreted are sometimes criticised on sociological and sometimes on theological grounds. Neither discipline can exist in a water-tight compartment without doing itself a disservice.[12] The interaction between the two disciplines is important and need not in any way be destructive either to Christian faith or to sociological understanding.

In addition to these general problems of the relationship

between sociology and theology there are some particular problems which relate to a sociology of the New Testament. The basic question concerns the reliability of the evidence given in the New Testament from which a sociologist would construct his interpretation. Modern theological scholarship has often concluded that this passage or that was not an original part of the text but a later addition. It has also argued, that the sayings of Jesus, were not the words of Jesus himself but those of the later church ascribed to Jesus by his followers. It is said that the early Christians were not deliberately dishonest but used an approach common in their world to deal authoritatively with particular problems they faced which Jesus himself did not encounter. Another recent theological concern has been with the way in which the editor of, say a particular gospel, has shaped material he has received in order to fit it in with his overall purpose or purposes in writing. The implication is that the moulding of the material in this way may in fact have altered the historical reliability of what was recorded.

These are important issues which occupy much of the attention of New Testament scholars and one needs to be aware of them in approaching the New Testament sociologically. It is not within the scope of this book to justify one's position on this matter. But it ought to be stated that the approach of the author is that of belief in the reliability of the New Testament documents as we now have them. The evidence they present, about themselves has been used to construct a sociological perspective, not naively, but on the assumption that what they claim about themselves is true, e.g., that the gospels really do record the authentic words of Jesus. Justification for this view must be sought elsewhere.[13]

One final theological issue needs to be acknowledged. Sociology tends to look for the common thread between movements. In so doing it is possible that it overstresses the similarities and underplays the differences between one movement and another. More of this will be mentioned from a sociological viewpoint later. But from the standpoint of the Christian believer it may have the effect of implying that his faith is not unique but merely one of a number of common human quests for God. Whilst it is recognised that even in church and missionary circles today the uniqueness of Christianity is being questioned, the author holds to the traditional Christian viewpoint that in Jesus Christ God has revealed himself to man in a unique and final way. What is unique however is the truth of Jesus Christ, both his words and his offer of a salvation achieved through the cross and resurrection. Sociologically he and his followers may share much in common with others. It is obvious that in other respects they share much in common with other human beings. Neither the original disciples nor present day Christians differ from other men in terms of their physical make-up, body chemistry or everyday language. So why should it be a matter of concern if they demonstrate common sociological patterns with other movements? The uniqueness may be maintained without the fear that sociological similarities will undermine it.

SOCIOLOGICAL PROBLEMS WITH THE NEW TESTAMENT

The difficulties in writing a sociology of the New Testament do not all lie on one side of the fence. A sociologist faces difficulties as well as a Christian believer.

To being with the sociologist does not have very much material to use as evidence for his theories. There is the New Testament itself and also other contemporary documents. But they were not written as sociological analyses and therefore they may not always be helpful in answering the questions which a sociologist wants to ask of them. He must be careful not to read too much into them. Eisegesis is a peril for the sociologists as well as the preacher! Further the number of documents he has are not numerous. If one was sitting down to write a sociology of the Second World War one would suffer from an abundance of material. But in this case the reverse is true.

A further problem lies, as already mentioned, in the fact that the models which a sociologist constructs tend to simplify reality. The sociologist is always interested in discovering patterns in the way in which men behave. The discovery of similarities leads him to the development of models and types. These are not even imagined to be replicas of reality. A model is sometimes deliberately constructed to accentuate certain features of the social phenomena in order that special attention can be paid to its significance. This is similar to what happens in a complex technical line drawing of an engine or even a map of the world where one part is isolated in a box in the corner of the page and drawn on a different scale in order that it might be seen with greater clarity.

When this procedure is applied to the New Testament it inevitably gives something of a distorted picture. Different models fit different parts of the development of the New

Testament. One example of this might be seen in relation to the question of authority. Sociologists speak of three pure types of authority: charismatic, traditional and rational–legal authority. It would be easy to simplify the complexity of the New Testament and argue that in the Gospels and some of the Acts charismatic authority is evident, whilst in the church of Jerusalem under James they were subject to traditional authority and in the Pastoral Epistles rational–legal authority has come to the fore. To do this would be to over-simplify each stage in the development of Christianity and to over-stress the diversity to be found in the New Testament. The very point of a pure type is that it never does exist in reality and the sociologist must always strive to be as faithful to reality as possible.

Historical sociology is a branch of the discipline that has special difficulties all of its own. Sociologists can usually support their theories by devising some way of testing them such as through surveys, interviews or participant observation. But for obvious reasons the members of a bygone age are not available to be investigated in this way! The researcher therefore has to recognise that his findings in historical sociology will inevitably be less assured than they would be in contemporary sociology.

A final difficulty has been mentioned by Howard Kee.[14] This is the danger of parallelomania. The danger arises when a superficial analysis of two institutions in two different cultures suggests that they resemble each other. It is an easy step from that to the conclusion that they are parallel phenomena. In fact their function may be very different in their differing contexts. Sweeping comparisons between the Graeco-Roman world and the home of the Gospels are not what is needed. What is needed is careful study of the New Testament itself before cautious conclusions are drawn.

CONCLUDING COMMENTS

The task of looking at the New Testament through sociological eyes is, then, fraught with pitfalls. There are traps both for the believer and the sociologist. Even so the immensely rewarding journey is worthwhile if we make it with our eyes open.

Above all we must recognise the tentative nature of our conclusions. There is no room for dogmatism but plenty of room for humility. Sociology itself is a tentative discipline and its relationship with the New Testament is even more uncertain.

Recognising that occasional attempts have been made at such a relationship at various times during this century it is still true to say that a significant relationship did not begin to blossom until the 1970s. Wayne Meeks,[15] whose writing is itself a sign of that relationship, believes that it is due to a discontent or restlessness with traditional approaches to the New Testament. Yet, as he says, if that is so, the concern for new approaches is a sign not of malaise but of vitality.

CHAPTER TWO

The Nature of the Jesus Movement

The spread of early Christianity is one of the most fascinating facts of ancient history. Historians debate how rapid its growth was and the precise path the growth took geographically. Others debate whether the spread, which resulted eventually in Christianity becoming adopted as the religion of the Roman Emperor, was good or bad for Christianity. For the sociologist the interest lies in another aspect of the same issue of growth.

Christianity has its roots in Galilee. The early disciples of Jesus were Galileans who were very much at home in a district of Palestine which, however one measures it, was quite backward in terms of civilisation. As the parables of Jesus show, his hearers were used to a world of farmers and fishermen; small-time landowners and petty kings. The village and the country suited them. By contrast the city, especially Jerusalem, was usually seen as a place where evil was done. The leading participants in the Jesus movement when it began were largely uneducated men who probably spoke Aramaic.

Yet the Jesus movement was to make little long-term impact in this area. Instead it was to grow and flourish in the more sophisticated parts of the Roman Empire. It was to take root in cosmopolitan cities, like Corinth, and to attract Greek-speaking followers. Later followers of Jesus came not from the peasantry but from a mixture of social classes. They were all at home in the world of the great Roman Empire.

It is this social transition which is of interest to the sociologist. The transition lies right at the heart of our concern with a sociological perspective of the New Testament because, as E. A. Judge has put it, 'The New Testament is itself a product of this shift. Its writers are mainly Jews of Palestinian associations; their readers the Greek-speaking members of Hellenistic communities.'[1] To that we may add that the synoptic gospels reflect one social context and most of the Epistles another whilst the Acts of the Apostles serves as a pivot between them. Our approach, then, will be to examine the progress of the Christian Church at a number of significant points in its development. First when it is an embryonic movement in the gospels; secondly, as the young church is born in Jerusalem and thirdly as it moves out from its early home to the rest of the Roman Empire. Finally, we shall study the church of the New Testament as it reaches organisational maturity. These glimpses will be like a number of still photographs which capture the growth of a child as he progresses toward manhood. Ideally a sociologist should be concerned with a movie picture rather than black and white still photographs, but even a movie is composed of a series of still pictures projected in rapid succession to each other. Perhaps, therefore, it is not too unsophisticated a framework in which to begin.

VARIATIONS ON A CONSENSUS VIEW

There is no full agreement about the sociological nature of the movement brought into being by Jesus. However, it is generally agreed that the movement should be interpreted as a millenarian movement, that is, a movement which arises in a time of unrest and which promises decisive social change. It will be described more precisely later in the chapter. This consensus view is often implicitly assumed by scholars rather than explicitly stated.[2] There are two recent works however in which the model of a millenarian movement is explicitly used. After introducing these particular works the chapter will then describe in depth the consensus model and its application to the Gospels. The chapter will conclude by questioning how suitable the concept of a millenarian model is for an understanding of the Jesus Movement.

A.   *Howard Kee: Community of the New Age*

Howard Kee's concern is to discover the purpose which lay behind the writing of Mark's Gospel. His very thorough search leads him to believe that Mark was produced by an apocalyptic community in Southern Syria probably in the years just prior to the fall of Jerusalem (AD 70). Its purpose was to act as a guidebook and as an exhortation to the members of the community who were travelling charismatic preachers.[3]

This conclusion may be questioned on theological grounds, but our interest lies in the fact that Kee's concern is to find a real social situation in which to fit the purpose of the Gospel. In exploring this concern he examines in some detail the nature of the supposed community. He does this partly by a detailed examination of the themes of the Gospel which he assumes to be reflecting the life-style of the community and also by comparing and contrasting this community with other contemporary communities of which we are aware.

The Jews had first had their spiritual and cultural distinctiveness corrupted by the inroads of greek civilisation and then, in the time of Jesus, been subject to the political dominance of Rome. For many Jews this had led to a feeling of impotence in the face of threatening forces. It had led to a moral and spiritual crisis in which they had asked how God could be true to his promises to David and still permit such events. It had provoked a crisis of meaning. Four responses can be observed to the Roman domination of Palestine. Some like Herod, collaborated; some like the Phaiisees, acquiesced but were ill at ease; some like the Essenes, opted out altogether and withdrew to the desert whilst others like the Zealots chose the path of insurrection.

The way of the New Community of Jesus was yet another option. It began as a pure community of followers of the prophet Jesus who came with a message of imminent and catastrophic judgment. Membership of the community was not limited to any one social or radical group but the demands made on the members were radical and transformed normal social and economic structures. They avoided political involvement because they considered it irrelevant. Instead Mark emphasises the special privilege of being a member of the community. Only its members can interpret the parables, witness certain of the miracles or be informed of the secrets of Jesus. Kee summarises the description of this elect esoteric community by saying:

> Its enemies are a blend of human, demonic and cosmic forces. It lives in hope of imminent vindication. The community was called together by a prophet sent from God; it will likewise be vindicated in the end-time by his agent.[4]

Kee really has two types of social group with which he compares the early Christian community. The major comparison must lie with other apocalyptic groups who believe themselves to be the secure elect who are about to witness or participate in an imminent vindication of their beliefs. In addition he also compares the wandering charismatic figures of, for example, Mark 6: 7–13, with the itinerant Cynic-Stoic philosophers who were active in the Hellenistic period. The Cynics urged men to reject the false values of their culture in favour of a simpler and freer life-style. The Stoics had a vision of an ideal society of Universal Brotherhood.

Both points of comparison have their strengths but it is with the first of these comparisons that the main sociological interpretation of the Jesus Movement lies. Kee, however, is not inclined to overstress either parallel since he is fully aware of the limitations of such comparisons. The distinctiveness of the community in Mark's Gospel is essentially that its members believe that Jesus of Nazareth is God's agent to bring the history of this age to a close.

B.   John G. Gager: Kingdom and Community

The second work which deserves mention is currently the most thorough and comprehensive sociological account of 'the social world of early Christianity'. Its survey spans the period from the origin of the Jesus Movement to its final acceptance as the religion of the Roman Empire. Gager's analysis of the gospels explicitly analyses the Jesus Movement as a Millenarian movement. As a result the exposition of the consensus view which follows owes much to him. His substantial contribution in other respects however merits attention. To begin with, Gager justifies the use of sociology as a means by which to understand the New Testament. He argues that history has so stressed the particularity of events that it has failed to see the common threads. Theology is likewise taken to task because its interpretations have been theoretical and only a few people engage in theorising. On the other hand Gager believes that sociology promises the possibility of seeing old facts in a new light now it has forsaken its desire to produce global interpretations of the world and has been prepared to settle for more limited models.

Following his analysis of the gospels Gager explores the way in which the followers of Jesus reacted when, as he understands it, the promises of Jesus regarding the ushering in of the Kingdom did not come true. His explanation makes use of the theory of cognitive dissonance which we shall examine in Chapter 4. The other centre of interest with the New Testament itself as far as Gager is concerned is the Book of Revelation. By the time this book was written Gager believes that the Christians had moved from belief in the coming of a material Kingdom of God to belief in the Kingdom as symbolic myth. The book of Revelation therefore speaks of convictions which are both deeply felt and enduringly held by man. These convictions are expounded in Revelation by the use of the alternating themes of victory versus defeat, freedom versus oppression and hope versus despair.

Leaving the New Testament itself Gager turns his attention to the way in which the millenarian movement began to stabilise. Among other features of organisational stability there is the fact that such organisations have usually defined what the beliefs and functions of the movement are. The process by which what is legitimate is clarified and what is illigitimate is rejected is not from Gager's perspective due to the inspiration of the Holy Spirit or due to the exercise of apostolic authority. Rather it is seen as the result of a process of social bargaining, even a power struggle, whereby various centres of interest within the initially diverse group crystallise their position vis a vis each other. The winners in this process become the holders of 'orthodox' views and the 'losers' become the heretics. This is not to imply that all conflict is negative. It is not. Some conflict is healthy and productive for the strengthening and unifying of the group and the more exact definitions of its boundaries.

In the next part of this work there is an examination of the relationship between the social structure of the Roman Empire and the social structure of the Christian Church as it developed over the first few centuries and became more acceptable to the higher classes. Finally, Gager asks what it was about Christianity that caused it to survive in the ancient Roman world when so many other religions died. He does not take it for granted that its survival implies that it was successful as a movement. He believes the question of its success is very much an open one. In the end, after a detailed examination of both internal and external factors which were relevant for its survival, he concludes that Constantine's conversion was not so much a matter of faith as of shrewd political judgment.

The Christian believer may find *Kingdom and Community* somewhat guilty of sociological reductionism in its conclusions. However, in its range and method Gager's work is a good example of the stimulation which can be gained from seeing the New Testament through sociological eyes.

THE CONSENSUS MODEL: A MILLENARIAN MOVEMENT

Millenarian movements are both numerous and diverse in history. In fact they are so numerous that one anthropologist can see them as the distinguishing feature of mankind. Kenelm Burridge claims '... the pain of the millennium belongs only to man. It is why he is man, why, when the times come, he has to make a new man.'[5]

It is not surprising therefore that millenarian movements have been a source of fascination for sociologists and anthropologists for decades. Such scholars have been eager to catalogue such movements in all their political and religious guises. A recent example of this is Bryan Wilson's work on the millenarian cults of Africa[6] in which he gives an amazing analysis of contemporary tribal and third-world protest movements which all fall within our general understanding of millenarian movement. However, he emphasises that a distinctive feature of these particular movements is that men are no longer prepared to wait for a millennium in the unspecified future—they long for it to dawn in the present. So they have welcomed more readily those movements associated with the working of miracles today rather than those which offer peace in the future.

When therefore Christianity is being interpreted as a millenarian movement it is not being relegated to some long lost shelf in the sociological museum. It is being compared and contrasted with movements which are still shaping the headlines in tomorrow's newspapers in many parts of the world.

In broad outline millenarian movements may be said to arise in situations of social unrest or where men are dissatisfied with their current social order. They promise the possibility of heaven on earth. This is to be brought about by the creation of a new man and a new social order together with the creation of new assumptions, attitudes and the renewal of all other aspects of man's social life. This new order is radically different from the existing order. The movement is led by a prophet who articulates men's longings, lives himself according to the new system and is instrumental in bringing in the new creation.

Other features may also be added. It is usually associated with a great release of emotional energy and can be a particularly creative period as far as religion is concerned.

Many such movements last for a relatively short period only. Indeed unless the millenium does arrive they can, by

definition, exist in their pure form for a brief period only unless they are remarkably successful in the sustaining commitment of their followers in the face of disappointed or post-
poned hopes.

Further, as Yonina Talmon has pointed out, the idea of a
millenarian movement is not necessarily related to the idea of
1,000 years as its relationship with the word millennium might
imply. Its attitude to time is the common factor in all millenarian movements, in that 'it symbolises the meta-historical
future in which the world will be inhabited by a humanity
liberated from all the limitations of human existence,
redeemed from pain and transience, from fallibility and sin,
thus becoming at once perfectly good and happy.'[7] The concept of a millenarian movement must not therefore be con-
fused with the theological idea of a millennium as mentioned
in Revelation 20.

Four major characteristics of a millenarian movement may
be isolated and their application to the Gospels examined.

A. *The Desire for Change*

Millenarianism arises when there is a widespread desire for
radical change within a society or within a segment of society.
Usually those who are seeking the change are disadvantaged in
comparison with others in their society in terms of their economic, political or social position. This disadvantage or deprivation does not actually have to exist and be measurable. If a
group within society feels itself to be disadvantaged it is
sufficient to cause its members to want to overcome these dis-
advantages by one means or another.

The Jews as a whole certainly felt deprived at the time of
Jesus. They had been politically disinherited by the Romans
and no longer really exercised any control over their own
affairs.

The alienation experienced by the Jews however was more
than just political. Bound inseparably with the political realities of their situation were moral and spiritual issues. It was
not just that men seemed incapable of exercising control over
their own affairs but God seemed to have deserted them.
Furthermore their inherited faith, which had promised to
secure the throne of David, seemed to have given but an
empty promise. More than this it appeared that evil ruled on
every hand. Violence, extortion, injustice, sickness and evil
spirits seemed to be in control. Small and humble men were
caught in a trap and became the objects of exploitation by

others. These evils seemed both unchallenged and unquench-
able.

Various reactions to this situation are evident among the
differing social groups of Jesus's day. The ruling classes
attempted to hold on to the shreds of power which remained
and so opted for a strategy of collaboration with the Romans.
The Pharisees accepted the situation with resignation, sometimes with uneasy resignation. They saw what had happened
as punishment from God for their nation's sins so they tried to
intensify the practice of their faith in order to appease an
angry God. Others like the Essenes decided that the nation
was so corrupt that they did not want to be part of it and withdrew to form their own pure community in the wilderness. A
few tried to topple the power of Rome by active military
opposition. The centre of this resistance was to be found in
Galilee among groups like the Zealots.

Did the Jesus movement relate to these feelings of oppression and the desire for change? There are many indications in
the gospels that it did. It is interesting to note that the Jesus
movement was largely seen as a Galilean movement in his own
day (Lk. 22:59; 23:6) and was thus seen not only as potentially
politically subversive but as having a bearing on the same
issues as gave rise to Zealotry.

More direct evidence of the desire for change is seen as one
surveys those who figure prominently in the ministry of Jesus.
Groups who had come to terms with their situation and interpreted it to their own satisfaction, such as the Sadducees and
Pharisees, are not among his followers but rather among his
opponents. When a rich man comes to discuss issues with Jesus
he goes away unconvinced (Mk. 10:17–22). In contrast when a
Roman Centurion does express faith in Jesus (Matt. 8:5–13) it
is a matter of comment and surprise. Usually the ministry of
Jesus is exercised among the sick, the outcasts, and the demon
possessed. Most of his time is spent with those whom others
had failed to help such as Zacchaeus (Lk. 19:1–10) a woman
who had been ill for twelve years (Matt. 9:20–22) and a man
deserted by his friends and relatives (Jn. 5:1–9). These all have
obvious personal need for a change in their lives.

In itself these lonely or sick individuals are not evidence of a
widespread desire for radical social change. There are always
such people suffering a personal deprivation of one form or
another. It does not mean that the disparate individuals are
necessarily the basis for a social movement. However, the
gospels clearly see them as symptomatic of the deeper problem of evil. Sickness, enforced loneliness or demon possession

are only signs of the total grip that evil had on the society of Jesus' time. So Jesus can place these problems side by side with deeper spiritual and moral problems and see the former as illustrative of the latter. Hence Jesus explained his mission by identifying himself with those who desired change. 'Those who are well have no need of a physician, but those who are sick; I came not to call the righteous but sinners' (Mark 2:17). The desire for change therefore was not limited to those who were manifestly sick but was to be found among those who were desiring to find spiritual wholeness as well.

A few of the disciples evidently wished to change their social situation. Among these one thinks of Simon the Zealot, Matthew the tax collector (remembering how unpopular tax collectors were) and maybe even Judas Iscariot. But what about the rest who like Peter, Andrew, James and John seem quite well set up in life before Jesus called them? Evidently they were not as settled as one would expect since Andrew and one other disciple had previously been attracted to the preaching of John the Baptist (John 1:35–42). Peter and his friends were certainly not among the poorest of the social group for they owned their own boats. But the economic changes of Palestine, as we shall describe them in the next chapter, would probably have rendered the lower middle classes, to which they belonged, uneasy about their financial position.

In addition as good, even if uneducated, Jews they would express concern about the future of their nation. It is this, rather than personal problems, that lies at the root of their desire for social transformation. Their repeated references to Jesus coming into or restoring his kingdom (Mk. 10:35–45; Lk. 22:24–38, 24:21; Acts 1:6) reflect this desire.

Further examination of the gospels, both in their characters and their teaching, would demonstrate even more the unrest that existed among the followers of Jesus. Such unrest however is only the first condition, even a precondition, of the formation of a millenarian movement. It is certainly not sufficient in itself to cause such a movement.

B. *A New Interpretation of Life*

Another essential component of a millenarian movement is that it offers people who desire change a new framework within which to understand their social experience and also the possibility of totally reinterpreting it in a new light. Thus, the hopeless of the earth may be offered hope in heaven; the poor may be viewed as spiritually rich and so on.

From the first page of the Gospels onwards it is evident that Jesus was to offer men just such a reinterpretation of their situation. Mary declared that through her conception of Jesus God had 'scattered the proud in the imagination of their hearts, . . . put down the mighty from their thrones and exalted those of low degree, . . . filled the hungry with good things and the rich he has sent empty away' (Lk. 1:51–53).

Jesus declared his own ministry in the same revolutionary terms:[8] proclaiming good news to the poor, release for captives, recovery of sight to the blind and setting at liberty the oppressed (Lk. 4:18). Similarly in his preaching he offered happiness to the poor, hungry, sorrowful and persecuted. Those who were happy by the normally accepted standards of his world receive no happiness from him.

The ability of Jesus to turn the world's standards and values on their head is seen most clearly in relation to a number of practical issues which are invariably the central concerns of men. Political power was of little or no concern to him. He was quite willing to pay taxes to Caesar (Mk. 12:13–17) because the issue of Caesar's authority failed to excite him. The reason becomes clear in the conversation Jesus had with Pilate during his trial (Jn. 18:33–38). The Kingship and authority of Jesus were of an altogether different order from that which men regarded as so prestigious.

Another issue to which reference has already been made is the attitude of Jesus to wealth. Some believe that there is to be found here 'a clearly formulated ethic of poverty'.[9] Others stress that Jesus did not actually condemn wealth as such but materialistic attitudes which made men slaves of mammon. Be that as it may it is true that Jesus stated that the wealthy would have difficulty in being members of his kingdom, (Mk. 10:23–27) whereas he gladly welcomed the poor and encouraged his disciples to leave everything to follow him. When he sent them out on a mission he commanded them to go without even the minimum means of protection or security (Mk. 6:7–12). The rewards for their loyalty to him however did exist. They were not the material rewards most people were after but the equally real and far more numerous alternative rewards which his disciples would receive 'now in this time . . . and in the age to come' (Mk. 10:29–31).

Most men take pride in their families. They belong to them, they find in them security and they are proud of their family traditions or connections. But here too Jesus presents men with a radical alternative. Normal family ties are replaced by the greater family ties that exist within the community of Jesus

(Mk. 3:31–34; 10:28–30 and Lk. 9:57–62). Even the single, the orphan and those without any good family connections can find a secure place in the family of God.

In relation to status Jesus also presents a radically different picture from that which would normally be accepted. He accepts and spends time with the non-entities. In fact he gives them a status as God's elect which far outstrips any status they would receive in this world. They alone have the mysteries of the kingdom revealed to them (Mk. 4:11 and 34). Even more, all of history is to be consummated as the elect are brought into his new Kingdom (Matt. 24:31). By contrast Jesus rejects the normal attitude to status as quite unhealthy for his disciples (Mk. 10:42–45).

Finally we might say that in regard to religion Jesus rejects the old and presents a vision of the new. He does this both in terms of religious morals as they had been codified by the Pharisees (Matt. 5:17–48) and in terms of religious ritual (Matt. 6:1–18) as it was usually observed.

In all these ways, then, Jesus criticises the old social attitudes and pattern of behaviour and presents a vision of a new community. It is to be a revolutionary community where 'the first will be last and the last first' (Mk. 10:31). It is to be 'the Kingdom of God', that is, the society in which God actively reigns. In it God's goodness, forgiveness, mercy and creative power rule, and the limitations of this life, hatred, exclusiveness, exploitation, pain and suffering are absent. Furthermore in preaching the possibility of this new order Jesus was not talking of a merely social dimension. His preaching looked forward to the radical recreation of man himself (Jn. 3:1–10).

C. *The Role of the Prophet*

Many situations exist in which men long for a fundamental social change and even have an idea as to what sort of society they would like without there coming into being a millenarian movement. What makes the difference? The answer lies in the existence of a prophet or charismatic leader. Gager has rightly warned that this should not be taken to imply that the prophet is the primary cause of the movement, rather he acts as a symbolic focus for the longings and creative energies that already exist.[10] The prophet articulates the strivings of the restless people. He provides the lens through which men can see their experiences in a totally different light. He himself becomes the symbol of the new man that he preaches. He also becomes the carrier of the message of the new man.

The concept of a prophet or charismatic leader within sociology has a long history. Max Weber[11] was the primary sociologist to develop and popularise the concept, basing his root ideas on the Old Testament prophets. It was Weber who reintroduced the word 'charisma' to our language before it was used by those within the church who had particular views on or experiences of the work of the Holy Spirit. Weber was not, of course, writing theologically. His intention was to outline the distinctive sociological features of religious charismatic figures in contrast to other religious leaders like priests.

The prophet was considered to be a man in touch with God as few or no others were in touch with him. He had a sense of calling from God and was accordingly a man with a mission. He viewed the situation in which he lived as a crisis and was able to offer authoritative answers to man's plight. To gain a hearing he did not rely on formal or recognised qualifications, such as a public office or academic status. He gained a hearing purely on the grounds of personal merit. He would often, too, authenticate his authority by resort to extraordinary means, such as the working of miracles. The prophet should not be viewed as an isolated figure. It was essential that his gifts and calling were recognised by others. Prophets became prophets because they had followers and even a band of disciples closely associated with them. The prophet would make exceptional demands on these followers. Even so the group would be bound together because of their personal loyalty to their master and through the vital emotion which the prophet's preaching generated.

It takes little imagination to apply this concept of the prophet to the person of Jesus. It could almost have been composed with him in mind. He was the bearer of new revelation from God and he was acquainted with God as no other Jew before him had been. Jesus alone called God 'Father'[12] (Matt. 6:9; 11:25; Mk. 14:36; Lk. 23:34, 46). The intimacy of his sonship brought him into a distinctive relationship with God.

From the time of Jesus' baptism on one becomes aware in the gospels of Jesus' sense of mission. It was a mission not only to proclaim the kingdom of God (Mk. 1:4) but also to go to Jerusalem and, when the time was right, to die (Mk. 8:31, 10:45; John 2:4, 7:6, 13:31).

The authority of Jesus is seen in his repeated use of the phrases 'but I say unto you' (Mt. 5:22, 28, 32, 34, 39 and 44) and of the emphatic 'I am' (Jn. 6:35, 8:12, 10:7, 11, 11:25, 14:6 and 15:1). Equally it is seen in his victories over the scribes and the Pharisees as they tried to trap him. The crowds we read, 'were astonished at his teaching, for he taught them as one who had authority, and not as the scribes' (Mk. 1:22).

Jesus did not rise to this position of public note because he had the benefit of, but precisely because he lacked the normal social, religious and educational means of advancement. It was a jibe hurled against him that he was only a carpenter's son from the backwater of Nazareth (Mk. 6:2–3). In spite of this, the authentication of his ministry lay in his transparent integrity, perceptive teaching and ability to work miracles of all kinds. Natural forces such as storms at sea, devilish forces like those who possessed the maniac of Gadara and human sickness were all seen to be subject to him.

The sociological component of the concept of the prophet is also evident in Jesus. Men left all, at his command, to follow him (Lk. 5:11, 27–28). In addition they were willing to endure discomfort while he was alive and to accept the prediction of suffering after his departure with tranquillity in order not to be separated from him. John makes it clear that Jesus was a prophet who made rigorous demands on his disciples (Jn. 6:60–66) very much as one would expect a charismatic leader to do.

Here, then, is another respect in which the Jesus movement seems to be a characteristic millenarian movement. Right at the heart of the movement stands an exceptional man, who wields the disenchanted individuals of this world into a movement who believe the Kingdom of God to be at hand.

D.   *Heaven on Earth*

The prophet who stands right at the heart of the millenarian movement has one other function. He is the agent through whom the new society will be brought into being. He is the instrument who will be used in the sight of all, to vindicate the discontented people who have chosen to follow him.

The belief in a new heaven and a new earth, in which all has been morally regenerated and in which the hoped-for conditions will really exist, is a distinguishing feature of millenarianism. Other men are content with different responses to the plight of the world. Some believe that the conversion of individual men will gradually change the world and so they seek to recruit others to their movement and to witness their change of heart. Others struggle to be the pure community themselves and so are compelled to withdraw from an evil world.[13] But a member of a millenarian movement believes that the total transformation of the world is on its way.

This feature of millenarianism makes it an unstable movement. Many have dreamt of the millennium but have failed to see it become and empirical reality. So when the hopes of millenarians have been disappointed the movement to which they have belonged has been forced to change in character. It may disappear altogether, but this is not as common a pattern as one would expect. Men often adapt their revolutionary thinking into more ordinary thoughts of reformation in which case they work within the system to bring about change. Or they may be happy to defer the expectation of total transformation in favour of more immediate benefits such as the working of miracles. More suprisingly the belief may persist or even intensify as will be explained in Chapter 4.

The existence of apocalyptic elements in the teaching of Jesus cannot be doubted. He announced that the Kingdom of God was 'at hand' (Mk. 1:14) and his parables spoke of the growth and triumph of the kingdom despite all appearances to the contrary (Mk. 4:26–32, 12:1–11). Repeatedly he sounded a note of finality and judgment (Mt. 25:1–13, 31–46). His teaching had a ring about it as if 'zero hour' was approaching.

The crowds believed that his new kingdom was about to begin and on one occasion after the feeding of the 5,000, they attempted to take him by force to make him king (Jn. 6:15). Similarly as he entered Jerusalem on a donkey he was greeted as the long-expected Messiah, the prophet who had been promised and a King who would restore the house of David (Matt. 21:1–11). His disciples likewise give the same impression of believing that it is an earthly kingdom that Jesus is about to inaugurate (Matt. 20:20–23, Acts 1:6).

There is also the manifest apocalyptic address recorded in Mk. 13:1–37 (and its parallels Matt. 24:1–51, Lk. 21:5–36). In these passages Jesus speaks about the end of the present scheme of history after certain events had been fulfilled. The ending is to be accompanied by events of cosmic proportions which will make it clear at the time what is happening even though the timing of these happenings cannot be known beforehand. Significantly, throughout the address Jesus gives guidance to his followers as to what to expect or do (Mk. 13:9, 14, 23) and 'the elect' are the ones for whose benefit the course of events is arranged (Mk. 13:20, 27). It is this focusing on the elect that makes the teaching of Jesus so typically millenarian.

AN ALTERNATIVE APPROACH

It would appear, from the exposition which has been given that the Jesus movement is a classic illustration of a millenarian movement. All the features one has learned to expect of such a movement are evidently of central significance to Jesus and his followers. For all that, it would be wrong to accept the conclusion that is was a millenarian movement too readily. No matter how plausible the analysis may appear it must be asked how faithful it is in its interpretation of the Gospels. When this question is put a number of problems immediately arise and three problems in particular may be mentioned.

First, this millenarian interpretation of the life of Jesus, of neccessity, overemphasises the eschatological aspect of his teaching. Secondly the view assumes, as a consequence, that Jesus did not expect his movement to continue after his death. Indeed since the kingdom would arrive prior to his death there would be no need to discuss such an issue. Thirdly, this view selects evidence of the radical nature of the teaching and ministry of Jesus to the neglect of evidence which presents Jesus in a more conservative light or as working within a more normal social framework.

It is possible, of course, to discount these problems as unimportant. John Gager, for example, argues that the existence of radical and moderate elements side by side in the Gospels is due to the fact that they do not reflect only the teaching of Jesus but the later teaching of his disciples as well. In his words 'the sources themselves span several generations and thus cover the time of initial apocalyptic excitement as well as the first phase of consolidation'.[14] In this case a view of the Jesus movement as a homogeneous millenarian movement is still possible. But on theological grounds it is a questionable approach. The presupposition that it was a millenarian movement can all too easily become the yardstick by which one judges what is of an early and what is of a later authorship. As a result anything which does not conform to one's sociological model can be relegated to the dustbin of secondary importance.

If however, on good theological grounds, one is prepared to reject this too selective approach to the Gospels and take the picture of Jesus which they present more seriously one must construct a slightly different sociological model to account for the Jesus Movement.

The quest for the historical Jesus has been one of the major areas of discussion in New Testament circles for well over a century. In the course of this long debate a work by Albert Schweitzer written in 1906[15] proved a sensation. Many scholars in the nineteenth century attempted to interpret Jesus as a contemporary liberal humanist but Schweitzer presented a totally different picture. He saw Jesus as a 'deluded dreamer' who had expected to establish imminently the Kingdom of God on earth. But, he argued, Jesus was to be disappointed. His death on the cross was an unexpected mistake which spelt the failure of his mission.

It is still very much this view with which sociologists build their models. Yet the quest for the historical Jesus has moved on apace since Schweitzer and has developed in a complex way.[16] Few serious New Testament theologians are prepared any longer to accept the inventive approach of Schweitzer to the life of Jesus. Why then are the sociologists prepared to continue to accept it? Any sociological models constructed must be built on good theological foundations.

That there were eschatological themes in the teaching of Jesus is readily accepted. What is not so readily accepted is that this was the overriding theme of his preaching to the exclusion of any preaching on how men ought to live in the here and now, prior to the creation of the new heaven and new earth. At times Jesus is patently conformist in his attitudes as for example when, unlike Peter, he is prepared to pay the temple tax (Matt. 17:24–27) or occasionally in his attitude to his mother (Lk. 2:51, Jn. 2:1–11 and 19:25–27).

Nor is it possible to accept that Jesus was deluded; taken by surprise by his own death at the very time when instead he had expected the kingdom to come. He clearly had perceived his own end for some time and had on several occasions accurately predicted it (Mk. 8:31–33, 9:31, 10:32–34). Whilst he clearly accepted the consummation of the new kingdom to be a sudden and catastrophic event, he also accepted that the kingdom was already present and at work within the world. As a result he resisted the attempts of his disciples to predict the date of the full coming of the kingdom (Mk. 13:32).

Further there is every indication that Jesus expected to be removed from the world before the millennial hopes would be fulfilled. To that end he commits the work of evangelism to his disciples (Matt. 28:18–20). The building of the church and the task of mission are not seen as after-thoughts; making the best of a failed dream when the messianic kingdom did not arrive. They are implicit in the teaching of Jesus throughout (Matt.

16:18, John 20:21). Jesus spent much time in the last days of his life privately instructing his disciples about the work they were to do after his departure from the world (Jn. 13:16 especially 13:19, 14:16–18; 16:4–15). It is in that light that the disciples themselves apparently interpreted their work as a continuance of the work of Jesus (Acts 1:1 and 28:31).

It is only possible to square this idea of continuity with the model of a millenarian movement by either saying that towards the end of his life Jesus had already realised he was a failure or by assuming that the whole idea is a later fabrication of the disciples themselves read back into the text.

Perhaps the most crucial difficulty with the millennarian model is that it overemphasises Jesus as a prophet and neglects altogether the view of Jesus as a Rabbi. This issue has been argued at some length by E. A. Judge[17] who concludes that the early Christians are more suitably seen as a scholastic community rather than a millenarian movement. Howard Kee has similarly argued that there are comparisons between the disciples of Jesus and the itinerant Cynic and Stoic philosophic communities as has been mentioned.

Judge points out that Jesus deprecates the title of Messiah probably because the popular idea of Messiah would have misled his hearers into the wrong kind of kingdom. Many saw Jesus as a prophet although this title was always a matter of controversy. Enemies and disciples alike, however, were willing to accept that Jesus was a Rabbi. It is also a title that Jesus himself seems happy to accept. He frequently taught in the synagogues (Matt. 4:23, 9:35). Moreover he was addressed as a Rabbi not only by the crowds (Luke 9:38, 12:13) and his disciples (Jn. 4:31) but by the Pharisees (Mt. 9:11); Sadducees (Mt. 22:23); a scribe (Mt. 8:19); the rich and the influential (Mt. 19:16, Lk. 18:18).

The calling, training and commissioning of a band of disciples is done in a manner typical of the way in which Rabbis worked. As a Rabbi he was a guest of Pharisees at their meal tables (Lk. 7:36, 11:37). He was supported by well-to-do women, including a member of the royal household (Lk. 8:2–3). In addition his burial was arranged by two members of the Sanhedrin (Jn. 19:38–39).

Judge concludes that although it is easy to make a social revolutionary out of Jesus this acceptance of him as a Rabbi must seriously qualify that view. At the last Jesus is condemned as a prophet but there was never any questioning that he had scribal authority that entitled him to be called a Rabbi. 'The Pharisees recognised a rival, but also a peer'.[18] After his death when his disciples took up the teaching role to which Jesus had called them they did so working through the normal channels of an established sect within Judaism.

By arguing in this way Judge does not wish to pretend that the apocalyptic elements in the teaching of Jesus did not exist. Rather he says, 'the early Christians were engaged in an attempt to win a regular status within the framework of the Jewish national life, while at the same time presenting the apocalyptic vision of Jesus' disciples'. This proved to be a source of tension which continued throughout the New Testament church; 'the tension of radical beliefs within a socially conformist sect devoted in the rabbinical manner to the study of the law'.[19]

The warning was given earlier that sociological models can sometimes simplify complex realities. In doing so sociology may unwittingly misrepresent the social phenomena it seeks to interpret. It has often done this with the movement founded by Jesus Christ. The consensus view has been that early Christianity was a millenarian movement although the assumption has often been more stated than examined. In many respects it was a millenarian movement. Jesus was a messianic figure who preached radically the coming of God's new kingdom. Even so that does not exhaust the whole of the picture. Millenarian movements do not usually persist—at least not recognisably in the form in which they started. The Jesus movement did persist. That alone should lead one to re-examine the nature of the movement. Judge's view that the early Christian sect was a typical scholastic grouping within Judaism has much to commend it and it is a healthy corrective to the consensus idea. Despite the untidiness of the approach perhaps it is more honest to accept that any sociologist viewing the Jesus movement should do so not from the perspective of one but from the perspective of both of these models.

CHAPTER THREE

The Growth of the Jesus Movement

Two models have so far been presented which provide a sociological interpretation of the Jesus Movement. The major
sociological approach has been to assume or argue that Jesus
and his followers were a typical millenarian movement. A
second model, which was entered as a corrective, is that of the
scholastic community. This chapter aims to extend the analysis
which has been given and it does so with particular reference
to the work of Professor Gerd Theissen.

Gerd Theissen is Professor of New Testament in the
University of Bonn and has contributed many stimulating
sociological insights into the New Testament. His insights are
not in any way limited to the Gospels but it is his work with
the gospels which concerns us for the moment.[1]

Theissen's view of earliest Christianity is that it was a
renewal movement within Judaism. By speaking of it as a
renewal movement Theissen is not advancing an entirely new
model—a third type—by which to interpret the gospels.
Renewal or revitalisation movements are often millenarian
movements under another guise. Here as elsewhere we are
simply encountering one of the problems which results from
the youthfulness of sociology. Unfortunately sociologists frequently use different labels for the same phenomena or analysis.

To describe the Jesus movement in the Gospels as a renewal
movement has the merit of stressing the continuity of the work
of Jesus with the religion of the Jews. It was in a Jewish context and very much from within Judaism that earliest Christianity grew. Such an analysis meets, in part at least, the objec-
tion of E. A. Judge to the overemphasis on the concept of Jesus
as a prophet which was mentioned in the last chapter. This

perspective inevitably leads to the conclusion, however, that judged on the basis of its own aims—to renew the Jewish Religion—the work was ultimately a failure. It did not succeed in revitalising Judaism but only in founding a new religion.

Initially the Jesus Movement did succeed as a renewal movement within Judaism and it is the explanation of this initial success which forms the central feature of Theissen's analysis which he develops from a Freudian perspective.[2] The Jesus movement grew originally in relatively peaceful soil, but soil in which any number of tensions can be discovered if one digs beneath the surface. These tensions were especially experienced by the Galileans. Jesus was successful because he both articulated the tensions and provided those who experienced them with an entirely new way of interpreting them. In this sense Jesus was a millenarian radical who stood the normal interpretations of the Jews on their head.

Why, then, did not this initial success continue? Theissen argues that it was because after the death of Jesus these tensions gave way to more open conflict within Palestine. When a conflict situation arises, as it did then, new movements do not usually flourish so easily. There is a regrouping of alliances against an external enemy so that even the more radical begin to seek refuge in the more traditional institutions.

In this way the followers of Jesus ceased to thrive within Palestine. Instead they began to develop in the very different social culture of other parts of the Roman Empire. Hellenistic society now welcomed them because they had a message which matched the Hellenistic social climate. Here there was peace, growing prosperity and flowering civilisation. New forces were at work overcoming out-dated national or social distinctions and a gospel which said that in Jesus Christ there was neither Jew nor Greek, slave nor free, was appropriate.

Besides examining in depth the factors which initially made the teaching of Jesus popular in Palestine Theissen also analyses the social organisation and structure of the Jesus movement. It is this issue we shall examine first.

THE ORGANISATION OF THE JESUS MOVEMENT

The Gospels give very little information about the structure of the Jesus movement. We know that Jesus was not intent on founding local communities and we are not going beyond the evidence if we make three further comments about it.

Central to the whole movement was Jesus himself. In the

hands of Theissen, however, this is not merely a repetition of the obvious point, already made, that central to all millenarian movements is a prophet. His abilities as a New Testament scholar lead him to look at the issue with care.

In doing so, Theissen sees that the crucial understanding of Jesus was found in the concept of him as the Son of Man. The title of Messiah would have led his disciples to expect a nationalistic and earthly king. The title Son of God would have led them to expect only divine activity in the world. Most frequently, however, Jesus calls himself the Son of Man. In this way the transcendent and immanent aspects of the work of Christ are combined. It further allows the suffering (usually associated with the Son of God) and victorious (usually associated with the Messiah) aspects of his work to combine in one person.

The relationship between Jesus and his followers is a parallel one. The experiences of the Son of Man and the demands made upon him will be their experiences and obligations too. Theissen produces a number of incidents of clear parallels between Christ and his followers. For example, he is Lord of the Sabbath (Matt. 12:8) and his disciples are therefore free from petty Jewish rules regarding the Sabbath (Matt. 12:1–2). Or again, he was homeless (Matt. 8:20) and so were they (Mk. 10:28). Persecution came his way and was to be expected by them. As he came to serve (Mk. 10:45) so they were to serve each other (Mk. 10:43, Jn. 13:12–17). Pointing to the future, however, the Son of Man was able to speak of the fact that his disciples would one day share in judgment with him (Matt. 19:28).

Their identification with the Son of Man becomes even more apparent when Jesus claims that by receiving or rejecting his disciples men will be receiving or rejecting himself (Matt. 10:14f, 40, Jn. 13:20). His solidarity with his disciples is such that at the final jdugment one's treatment of the disciples is considered to be the same as one's treatment of Christ himself (Matt. 25:31–46).

To be like Christ was therefore a very real and practical quest for his disciples. Not all, however, were able to be identified with him to the same extent. This leads Theissen and others[3] to conclude that there was in fact a two-tier system of discipleship under the Son of Man.

The upper tier consisted of the wandering charismatics. These disciples are seen as the most fully committed to Jesus. They share with him in the insecurity of homelessness (Matt. 8:20, Mk. 6:7–13), of having left their family (Lk. 14:26) and of having renounced possessions (Mk. 10:17ff and Matt. 6:25–32). Moreover these features are not merely mentioned in passing but given special emphasis in the Gospels. These disciples place such complete faith in Jesus that they are even prepared to forego any elementary means of security on their journeys (Mk. 6:8f) and to turn the other cheek when attacked (Matt. 5:38–42).

Theissen believes that their ability to leave home and become wandering disciples reflects the extreme conditions under which they must have been living. It also points to a rural background. Such men were probably not artisans or they would have taken the tools of their trade with them. Farmers and fishermen, however, are limited as to where they can work. So when they followed Jesus they inevitably left all to do so.

Furthermore such itinerant preachers in any society would be 'outsiders'. Their ethical radicalism would have made them such. As Theissen says, 'They had a few sympathisers scattered about; but it is not difficult to visualise what the majority thought of these people without homes or jobs who made the common people uneasy by their preaching of an imminent end of the world, who could already see those towns who rejected them going up in fire.'[4]

At the start of the movement these men were at its heart. They became the apostles, prophets and teachers of the very early church and at the early missionary work was centred on them. In spite of that, Theissen shows how their place became less central as the church grew and especially as it became acceptable in the cities. The cities demanded some form of organisation and wandering charismatics do not easily fit into stable organisations. Furthermore, as the gospel was accepted by more and more people so its radicalism was toned down, in order that it might become more acceptable.

The lower tier of discipleship consisted of sympathisers who were rooted in local situations. Theissen says that they had no rationale in themselves but can be understood only 'in terms of their complementary relationship to the wandering charismatics'.[5] Included in this group were Peter's family (Mk. 1: 29ff); Mary and Martha (Lk. 10:38ff); Simon the leper (Mk. 14:3) and various women (e.g., Lk. 8:2). Their role was to provide a base and support for the wandering disciples.

Even among these people Theissen tries to detect a latent willingness to leave home. But the evidence for this is lacking. It is true to say, on the other hand, that as disciples of Jesus, although they continued to live in normal society and practise normal Jewish worship and ritual, they brought to that norm a new perspective and a new ethical code which was derived from Jesus (e.g., Mt. 5:23).

The picture of the early Jesus movement is drawn with bold strokes. To be really true to the gospel narratives other gentler lines need to be added to it. To begin with, although it is true to say that there were two groups among the disciples, those who were itinerant and those who were settled, some of the implications drawn do not necessarily follow. Theissen implies that the itinerants occupied a superior spiritual position. They were closer not only to their Master and his life-style but to his intentions as well. The settled disciples have any place in the structure at all only because the itinerants exist. The settled disciples have not been able to come to terms with the radical demands made by Jesus to the same extent as the itinerants. It is certainly true that Jesus demanded much of his followers and was not happy for people to join his group in any half-hearted way (Lk. 9:62; 14:28). In fact he actively discouraged mass discipleship which was merely the result of large group dynamics at work (Jn. 6:60–71). Contrary to Theissen, Jesus demands perfection of all his disciples, not just the elite (Matt. 5:;48 cf, Matt 19:21).[6] Even so Jesus equally clearly did not demand that every person he met and helped should become itinerant with him. Lepers and many others in the gospel were healed and then sent back to the local priest, who acted as the medical officer of health, and to their families. They had become as aware of the Kingdom of God as the itinerant disciples had. In one case, that of Legion, Jesus expressly forbade him to join his wandering band of disciples (Mk. 5:18f). The call of God for him was to to return home and tell others what Jesus had done. Surely this was no lesser discipleship for him. Jesus nowhere indicates that those in the settled homes which he visited were less worthy of him than those who were totally committed to him as itinerants. Over and above all that it must be remembered that the same Jesus whose teaching is often presented in an exclusivist light could also be very inclusivist. When the disciples protested about a man who was not of their number conducting exorcisms, it was Jesus who said, 'Do not forbid him, for he that is not against you is for you' (Lk. 9:49f).

In identifying the two-fold stucture therefore it is wiser not to imply that spiritual superiority or inferiority existed; only that two patterns of discipleship can be discerned.

In addition to this we must note that part of Theissen's argument is that although originally radicalism was at the heart of the Jesus movement it was soon lost as the church developed and was replaced by behaviour and demands which were more acceptable to 'normal' people. Such a displacement of radicalism can be discerned if one compares the church of the later Roman Empire with the early disciples. But it is too easy to overstress this contrast and to create a discontinuity where it does not exist.

A more unified view is to be found within the New Testament and the *Didache*. Here radical and less radical elements exist side by side. This tension begins in the Gospels, is evident in the Acts, and persists throughout the Epistles. From Jesus onwards the church never gives unbridled expression to either radicalism or conservatism. In the later epistles of Paul the settled church leaders receive a fair amount of attention. Even so the place of itinerant preachers is still very much in evidence. In the very process of interpreting the ethical demands of the Gospel for a new cultural situation the tone of voice with which they are spoken inevitably changes. In essence, however, the demands do not change. The church of the later New Testament has more in common with the disciples of the gospels than some recent scholars have been prepared to admit. And Theissen's analysis of the structure of the Jesus movement should not be used as another plank in the argument that what Jesus taught and what the later church practised were two different things.

FACTORS WHICH AIDED THE GROWTH OF THE MOVEMENT

The central part of Theissen's work *The First Followers of Jesus* contains a very useful analysis of four factors which enabled the Jesus movement to grow. They are all features of the wider society and he is able to demonstrate not only how they affected those who eventually became followers of Jesus but also parallel responses made by others.

Firstly, there were *socio-economic factors*. At the time of Jesus, Palestine was undergoing a period of rapid social transition. A number of natural phenomena, e.g. the famine of 25 AD when even Herod was moved to melt the palace plate for the poor and the epidemic of 29 AD combined with the probable over-population of Palestine and problems in the distribution of goods to produce social upheaval. This was aggravated by the fact that the commercial activity of the Pax Romana had led to changes in the social structure of Palestine. Those connected with the family of Herod rose through the social ranks; some scribes became upper class and so joined the older aristocratic families in status and wealth became concentrated in the hands of a few. Lk. 19:11–27 reflects this background.

The effect of these changes was to dislocate some from their social situation. The rootlessness which was caused is reflected in the gospels in its reference to a number of beggars or robbers. Other rootless people chose to overcome their problem by joining a religious community such as that at Qumram whilst others sought to change their situation by joining the resistance fighters. These movements in the social classes shattered the traditional values and made men cry out for a renewed nation. Since those who were squeezed most were those on the edge of the middle class they were ripe to be wielded into a new social movement who would be active in the service of God. It is this section of society from which the disciples of Jesus chiefly came. A lower social group, as history repeatedly illustrates, might well have moved in the direction of more direct political rebellion.

Secondly, there were *socio-ecological factors*. The Jesus movement took root in the hinterland of Judea and as we have seen was chiefly a rural or village phenomena. Being on the borders of the territory the Galileans would be subject to more outside influences than those at the heart of the nation and their potential for revolt was well known. They would also demonstrate much more independence of mind than those closely locked into the life of the nation. Further, as the parables reflect, they were probably used to experiencing the economic pressures which arose from having absentee landlords.

This factor is demonstrated positively, in that Jesus derives most of his support from Galilee, and negatively in the attitude of the gospels towards Jerusalem. The attitude of Jerusalem however, is never wholly negative. Paradoxically it is, for the followers of Jesus, always essentially a holy city. Nonetheless, it is the city where Jesus is put to death. Throughout his life he looks in its direction aware that it would spell his crucifixion. At the end it would be unwelcoming to him and reject him.

This theological judgment on Jerusalem is paralleled by the social judgment which the followers of Jesus would have sensed. There was no real commercial class in Jerusalem. Its livelihood was totally dependent on the temple and allied business. So the inhabitants of the city had vested interests in not upsetting the peace that Rome had brought in case it meant the end of their means of support. The dwellers in Jerusalem were therefore conservative unlike the independently minded village dwellers who followed Jesus. To some extent therefore the Jesus movement reflects not only the economic tensions which existed but the rural versus urban tensions as well.

Thirdly, there were *socio-political factors*. The crises that existed in Palestine is clear. It expressed itself politically in the unceasing quest for the right balance of power. Three centres of power vied with each other. The older aristocratic families as encapsulated in the High Priests vied with the new Roman client rulers of Herod's family and together they jostled for power with the Roman procurator. Something of this political power game can be seen during the trial of Jesus.

The crux of the problem as far as God-fearing Jews were concerned was that the old representatives of the theocracy were no longer apparently in effective control. What then did theocracy mean; if it meant anything at all? They all knew, as Jesus stated, that a kingdom divided against itself cannot stand (Mk. 3:24f) so what had happened to the kingdom where God had once ruled? These tensions gave rise to another quest – the quest for a real theocracy, one which would be effective. Again it was this need which Jesus was meeting in his preaching about the Kingdom of God. It spoke of a future kingdom where the reign of God would be evident to all. At the same time it spoke of the present activity of God within his world which no alternative governmental forces could prevent.

Lastly there were *socio-cultural factors*. The whole Jewish culture was now under threat. How could the idea of their special covenant relationship with God mean anything in the light of their recent national experiences? They were experiencing, in other words, a crisis of identity. What did it really mean to be God's people now? Many saw their experiences as God's way of punishing them for their sin. Having reached that conclusion, the issue for them was to decide how to behave in the light of their punishment. Theissen argues that various groups reacted in different ways in respect of two sets of norms. Some, e.g., the Pharisees argued that the norms should be observed more rigidly and more generally within society. In other words they were trying harder to please God. So they spelled out in minute detail just how the ordinary Jew should observe the Torah. The Essenes also intensified both sets of norms but kept their strict observance to an elite group who withdrew from the wider contaminated society. The restistance movements relaxed the social norms but made the religious norms more rigid.

Early Christianity too was a response to this identity crisis. The Christians' response to the quest for the discovery of the true Israel was to intensify some norms and relax others. Norms about one's behaviour were made more demanding and even internalised (e.g., Matt. 5:21–48). On the other hand norms concerning religious ritual were relaxed (Mk. 7:1–13). This relaxation of norms is particularly seen in the way in which all men, whatever their social standing or nationality became acceptable as members of the renewed community. The true Israel was now defined in terms of one's attitudes to Jesus of Nazareth, not in terms of one's ancestral blood.

Gal. 4:4 claims that Jesus was born of Mary 'when the time had fully come'. This has long been interpreted by Christians as meaning at least in part when the circumstances were right. Usually the circumstances referred to are the unified language; the excellent road system and the relative peace brought by the Roman Empire. Theissen exposed other factors—factors of sociological significance—which demonstrates just how ripe the time was for the message Jesus came to bring. Whether consciously exploited by Jesus or not, the sociological factors Theissen identifies aided the growth of his movement.

Reference must be made in conclusion to the final contribution Theissen has made to our understanding of the work of Jesus. The existence of tensions in the crisis situation we have outlined not only gave rise to the search for new solutions but also produced aggression. From a Freudian standpoint Theissen has shown how the Jesus movement dealt with that aggression. Men felt aggrieved at their situation and wanted to hit out, maybe even against God himself. Jesus taught them to turn these aggressive feelings into the opposite emotion and to love instead of hate. He also provided them with compensation for their aggression. Instead of Rome the aggrieved were taught to transfer their aggression to demons. They could find too a scapegoat in the crucified Son of God. Moreover there was to be a final judgment day when God's ultimate acts of righteous vengeance would take place. This also enabled a person who felt oppressed to turn the aggression into a boomerang and bring it to bear on the one who had originally oppressed him.

Jesus then, did not become a messianic figure simply because of his own exceptional personal qualities. He was a messiah because of that and because of the social context in which he lived. Many were searching for new meaning and a new pattern of religious and social life. It is as Matthew records, 'When he saw the crowds he had compassion for them because they were harassed and helpless, like sheep without a shepherd' (9:36). Jesus became the true shepherd of a new Israel.

CHAPTER FOUR

The Early Church in Jerusalem

It is one of those curious twists which characteristically occur as organisations develop that a group of Jesus' disciples should make their headquarters in Jerusalem. None of them came from Jerusalem and, as has been mentioned, the teaching of Jesus may well have given expression to their Galilean, anti-urban feelings. Jesus had given orders that they were to wait in the city after Pentecost (Acts 1:4) and his disciples were obedient to him. They then continued to live there even after the Holy Spirit had come. Reading the Acts it seems as if they would almost have been content to remain there as an enclave of the Kingdom of God on earth, had it not been that the Holy Spirit used persecution as a means of forcing them apart (Acts 8:1). From that time on the localised urban sect consciously became a great international fellowship. Its numerical growth and geographic spread inevitably involved corresponding sociological developments.

Scholars have been in hot debate for some time over the trustworthiness of Luke's record of the early church, but there are good reasons for believing the Acts of the Apostles to be historically accurate.[1]

Fortunately, therefore, there is much historical data which can be used as a foundation for a sociological interpretation of the early church's life. Even so, it must be used with care, remembering that the Acts was not written with the object of being a sociological report. Many sociological issues, therefore, inevitably remain obscure.

THE DEVELOPMENT OF THE EARLY CHRISTIAN SECT

With the removal of Jesus from the scene the millenarian movement began to look much more like what sociologists call a sect. That is to say, it was a voluntary religious organisation with clearly marked boundaries whose members joined because they underwent the initiation of baptism. The group had high behavioural standards which led to severe censure on those who contravened them. They saw themselves as the exclusive recipients of the Holy Spirit. Further, they were indifferent to, and sometimes in active opposition to, the recognised state and religious authorities. Under this general description of a sect, a number of different types of sects can be distinguished[2] and several of these types can be seen in the early church in Jerusalem.

Until the day of Pentecost the bewildered disciples of Jesus were not concerned to gain recruits for their movement. They were an *introverted group* or as sociologists would say an *introversionist sect*, whose sole activity was to pray (Acts 1:14). Even so, they were conscious of their status before God and knew that they must prepare for change in role. Consequently, they agreed to make the number of apostles up to twelve again, so that they could be ready for action. The qualifications on which they insisted for the new apostle—that he had been involved in the Jesus movement from John until the Resurrection—meant that it was almost inevitable that Judas' replacement would be a Galilean. The introversion of the movement was therefore strengthened.

All that changed dramatically, however, on the Day of Pentecost. From that day onwards they actively sought to convert others in their way. Initially their only platform was Jerusalem, but it was a good platform. Men and women from all over the ancient world were there and were converted. As a result, the movement spread rapidly. Every *conversionist sect* applies some test to potential members. For the God-fearers who were in Jerusalem the most obvious test that they had received the Holy Spirit was to demand public baptism of them (Acts 2:38, 41).

Following their conversion, new patterns of behaviour and aids to piety were embraced (Acts 2:42). It is evident from the story of Ananias and Sapphira (Acts 5:1–11) that the standards were rigorously enforced. Such enforcement serves to keep the boundaries between member and non-member clear. It was no light matter to be a member of the early church. The circumstances simply did not permit the half-hearted identification with the church which is common in our day (Acts 2:43, 5:5, 11, 19:17).

It is generally assumed today that such a strong religion is unlikely to flourish. It is argued that to make strong and comprehensive demands on potential converts and to create a distance between the convert and non-convert purposely would lead to the alienation of potential converts with the result that the movement would not survive for long.

Surprisingly, the evidence, both ancient and very modern, suggests quite the reverse.[3] 'Strong' religions, such as that of the early disciples in Jerusalem, often show remarkable growth.

Another problem of conversionist sects is that their very desire to win converts brings them into such close contact with the unconverted that their message and life style is eventually diluted or in time altogether neutralised. At Jerusalem this did not appear to be a problem; the reason being that even though they were a conversionist sect they had strong utopian overtones.

David Martin has picturesquely described such a sect as 'a colony of heaven (where) the world outside is an untidy garden within which sin and corruption rage.' There is evidence that this was how the early disciples viewed their position in the world in Peter's first sermon on the day of Pentecost (Acts 2:40). The development of a common possession of goods which followed is also typical of what would be expected of a utopian sectarianism.

Community living serves a number of functions. Since it ensures, at least for a short time, that its members are adequately provided for, it serves to isolate them from the wider society. It enables them to express tangibly their togetherness. Its group cohesiveness acts as a powerful reinforcing agent to the group's beliefs. It may also be that the group consciously come to consider themselves as a foretaste of the social life of heaven. Utopian sects usually have a strong emphasis on eschatology and see themselves as playing a significant role in the ushering in of the new world.

Just how extensive the idea of the community was among the early Christians is a moot point. Clearly they exhibited a high degree of solidarity. Luke (Acts 2:42–47, 4:32–37) seems to indicate that all were involved in the pooling of their resources. On the other hand, in the incident of Ananias and Sapphira it is stated that there was no compulsion on them to put their goods into the common purse (Acts 5:4). Ernst Haenchen also argues that 'the good deed of Barnabas (Acts 4:36, 37) only survived in memory because it was something out of the ordinary, not the rule.'[5]

It is generally accepted that the belief that Jesus was soon to return led his disciples to organise this primitive type of communism. By its very nature it could not have been a long-term project. They only pooled their resources and there was no attempt to organise any co-operative trade or production to ensure a flow of finance. So, when the initial capital ran out, they were bound to be in trouble.

From other parts of the New Testament (Acts 11:27–30, Gal. 2:10, Rom. 15:26) we know that the Jerusalem church, after these initial days became quite poor. Their experiment in primitive communism has often been held responsible for their subsequent poverty. Some believe it to have been an unwise move for this reason. However, it is more likely that the Church in Jerusalem was condemned to a life of poverty irrespective of this. Hengel explains it as a result of 'pressure from the Jewish environment and the famine under Claudius during the forties.'[6] Bruce further argues that Jerusalem as a city was not economically viable and had no alternative but to rely on gifts from faithful Jews and the income derived from pilgrims.[7] It was inevitable that the church should share in this economically precarious position and that, as it was distinguished more and more from the temple, it should suffer even more severely.

Some see great theological significance in this pattern of organisation. It is true that it provided early Christians with one of the most concrete ways of expressing their equality and fellowship. But, as far as the rest of the New Testament is concerned, there does not seem to be anything spiritually superior about it or anything specifically Christian about its structure. It is more probable that in its very early and enthusiastic days it was an obvious pattern of organisation for the church.[8] It was a natural extension of the idea of the common purse which Jesus and his disciples kept (John 12:6).

This embryonic communism soon began to show some strains. Luke presents a very unified view of the church in the opening chapters of the Acts. Chapter 6 however opens, without prior warning, with a record of the church's first potential division. As with most disputes, it is unlikely that this was the first and only grievance that involved members of the early church. It is more probable that it was the issue which brought underlying grievances to the surface.

The church had enjoyed a period of rapid expansion and as a result it was no longer as culturally monochrome as it had been at the start. Hellenists were being converted. They were Greek-speaking Jews of the Dispersion; a far cry from the plain Galileans. Many Jews looked upon Hellenists as being not quite pure Jews, and within the church some of that attitude may well have still persisted even though they were accepted as equals in Christ. Hill cites evidence that since the dispute concerned the distribution of food 'the Hebrews had not recognised the "ritual cleanness" of the Hellenistic widows in respect of dietary laws.'[9] That may be so, but even if not, it is not hard to understand how the original members of any rapidly expanding group felt threatened by the new-comers.

To meet the problem a major step forward in organisational development was suggested. The existing leadership structure was considered to be inadequate and a new group of leaders were chosen. It is often thought that these seven men were a second tier in the leadership hierarchy with more mundane functions to pursue than the apostles (Acts 6:3, 4). Luke, however, goes on to show them in an altogether different light. They are not subsequently seen as table-waiters but as preachers and missionaries. Some scholars have therefore concluded that they did not form a group beneath the apostles but alongside of them – a distinct ethnic leadership group.

The strong coherence of the small band of Jesus' disciples was therefore now broken. Luke records how through the preaching of Stephen a persecution arose which caused the Hellenistic Christians to scatter from Jerusalem (Acts 8:1). From then on international evangelism took place and Jerusalem, whilst it remained the centre of control in the church, had to work hard to maintain its leadership. Furthermore, the Christians of Jerusalem became known as 'the Poor'.

DEVELOPMENTS IN AUTHORITY

Sociologists have in general followed the types of domination which were first defined by Max Weber.[10] Weber spoke of types of 'domination' because domination is a more inclusive concept than authority. The word domination implies that when a command is given it will be obeyed. Authority also implies obedience but obedience which arises out of voluntary compliance, or the self-interest of the obedient person or some agreement about the legitimacy of the command. In the light of this distinction when we discuss the New Testament we may do so in terms of authority rather than dominance.

Weber distinguished three types of domination in pure forms. Firstly there was the charismatic type of domination which we have already referred to in relation to the life of Jesus.[11] Secondly there was traditional domination which can be seen in its purest form in ancient patriarchal families. Thirdly there was a later form of domination called legal domination which was based on the rule of law.

Christianity had its origins under charismatic leadership. But charismatic leadership is the most unstable form of authority there is since it centres on the personal qualities of the leader himself. Any group therefore which expresses loyalty to this leader is bound to pass through a vulnerable stage when the charismatic leader leaves the scene. The early Christians were no exception.

Naturally leadership passed into the hands of those who had been most closely associated with Jesus during his ministry. To some extent they were charismatic figures in their own right. Luke emphasises their bold public leadership even though they lacked the usual qualifications for leadership (Acts 4:13). He also emphasises the many extraordinary deeds they did (Acts 3:1–10, 5:12–13). Such deeds are commonly done by charismatic leaders in order to legitimise their position.

In spite of this the apostles were not, in sociological terms, pure charismatic figures. Their charisma derived only from their relationship to Jesus. They were not originating anything themselves; only continuing what their master had done (Acts 1:1). So the charisma lost its purity and began to be modified. Charisma loses some of its potency as soon as it is passed on to a second generation of leaders; as soon as they begin to share it with others and as soon as they secure their place more firmly in the structure of the group. This process is referred to as the institutionalisation of charisma.

One example of this process can be seen in the election of Matthias to fill the place left vacant by the suicide of Judas Iscariot. The chief qualification which was demanded of Judas' replacement was that he had been with the Jesus movement from its earliest days (Acts 1:21–22). Incidentally, that almost certainly meant that the election of another Galilean was about to take place. More significantly it meant that the individual's own personal qualities were not uppermost in the minds of the group. Matthias would certainly have had such qualities. Eusebius, the early church historian, claims that Matthias was among the seventy sent out by Jesus on a mission, but it was not primarily his personal charismatic qualities for which he was being chosen.

The choice of the seven Hellenistic leaders (Acts 6:1–6) is a further example of institutionalised charisma. These men were no ordinary men. They were chosen for their exceptional

qualities as men 'of good repute, full of the Spirit and of wisdom'. But they were not in a sociological sense pure charismatic leaders. Pure charismatic leaders emerge or erupt onto
the scene; they are not elected to office by others.

In this respect the apostle Paul must be seen as a charismatic
leader. He was personally called by God (Acts 9:15; Gal. 1:15)
and only subsequently had this call confirmed by either
Antioch or Jerusalem. His life-style, ministry and miracles
were all 'extraordinary'. He was very conscious of his task and
position. Churches which he founded recognised his 'apostleship' and consequently his authority over them. Even so Paul
was not a pure charismatic. He was neither the saviour of the
churches he founded nor was he establishing something new.

Paul's relationship to the charismatic leaders at Jerusalem
too is interesting. Bengt Holmberg has written a very
thorough essay, using Weber's categories of analysis, on the
relationship between Paul's authority and the authority of
Jerusalem. He concludes that 'Paul and the church of Jerusalem stand in relations of mutual but not symmetric independence and responsibility.'[12] Jerusalem clearly maintains its
pre-eminent position because of its closeness to Jesus. Paul's
authority was limited to areas not already under the influence
of Jerusalem.

In addition Holmberg argues that Paul was an example of
routinised charisma rather than pure charisma for a number of
reasons.[13] As well as being a man of power Paul displays himself to be a man of great weakness. He distinguishes between
himself and his gifts in such a way as to cause people not to be
devoted to him personally. His attitude to money is pragmatic
and rational. He is prepared to organise his churches. And,
above all, as he himself emphasises, he is not an originator of a
new movement but the transmitter of already formed traditions (1 Cor. 11:23). None of these characteristics fits the
'pure' charismatic, so by the time that Paul had established his
churches the pure charisma of Jesus had already been institutionalised in Jerusalem and routinised in Paul himself.

The church then, in sociological terms, was largely in its
early days a charismatic group of the second generation. However, even in the Acts one other form of authority can be
detected. James, the brother of Jesus, became a leader of the
church in Jerusalem (Acts 12:17, 15:13). Eusebius later tells us
that he was appointed to the office of the first bishop of Jerusalem by Christ himself. We know little of James except that
he died a martyr's death at the hands of the High Priest
Ananias in AD 61. Josephus informs us that his stoning pro-

voked a public outcry because he was so much respected for his piety.

What was the basis of James' authority? The apostles were chosen because of their closeness to Jesus. The Hellenistic leaders were chosen because of their abilities. James was among those chosen on the basis of ascription, not achievement. His appointment was most probably due to the fact that he was the brother of Jesus. The position he assumed after the death of his brother was typical of the way in which the next oldest brother would assume the status of the deceased in the family. So James' appointment is in all probability an example of traditional authority. The early Christians saw little reason to construct entirely new forms of organisation when existing Jewish models were to hand.[14]

That such traditional authority was in operation in this case is further supported by the statement of Hegesippus that on the death of James a cousin of Jesus assumed the leadership and that the blood relations of Jesus enjoyed a special and privileged position within the church.

THE SOCIAL CAUSES OF PERSECUTION

The infant church in Jerusalem soon became familiar with opposition and persecution. From the perspective of the early believers the opposition arose because men continued to reject Jesus of Nazareth and his message. From another perspective, however, it is possible to detect social factors also influencing the opposition.

An analysis of Luke's statements regarding the opponents of early Christianity in Jerusalem contains some surprises. Nearly all the opposition is attributed to the Sadducees or those associated with them (Acts 4:1, 5:17, 6:12, 23:6–9). On one occasion the source of the opposition was the Synagogue of the Freedmen (Acts 6:9) and on another occasion the source of opposition was Herod (Acts 12:1ff). The surprise is that the Pharisees, who were the constant irritants of Jesus, are not directly involved with the persecutions at all, with the exception of Saul of Tarsus.

Jeremias' careful study of *Jerusalem in the Time of Jesus* enables us to interpret these bare statements of fact. It is usually thought that the Sadducees were a party of the priesthood. Jeremias, however, produced evidence to show that they were both priestly and lay and in either case they were the nobility. Many of them must have been members of the privileged and landowning families. They were men of dignity, importance and influence. The chief priests were generally Sadducees. Moreover, the Sadducees dominated the council. Jeremias concludes that, 'the patrician families of the Sadducees formed a tightly closed group, with an elaborate tradition of theology and doctrine, they kept strictly to the exact text of Scripture, which shows the conservative character of these circles.[15]

It is not hard to deduce from this why they would oppose the early Christians. As conservatives they would dislike the disciples' radicalism and enthusiasm. As members of the nobility they would dislike any potential disturbers of the status quo who might threaten their vested interests. And as literalists when it came to Scripture, they would certainly not have been able to convince themselves that a crucified person was the Messiah.

Herod would have shared some of their reasons for wishing to do away with the Christians. He, too, had a position to protect which the new group might disturb. His position, however, was very much dependent on the goodwill of Rome which he had already forfeited on previous occasions and so he could ill afford to do so again. Whilst the followers of Jesus had been content to remain a Jewish sect they were popular with the people in general. But it seems that once the gospel was offered to non-Jews they forfeited this popularity. Herod's persecution (Acts 12:1ff) did not take place until the Jewish Christians had begun to fraternise with the Gentiles and Samaritans. So when he persecuted them it was, on his part, a well-timed political move which had the effect he had hoped for in advancing his own popularity.

The Pharisees are presented in a good light in the Acts of the Apostles. It was a Pharisee, Gamaliel, who urged caution when Peter and John were being tried before the council (Acts 5:34). Pharisees are named as among the believers who attended the Jerusalem council (Acts 15:5), even if they were not keen to encourage the non-Jewish tendencies in the Church. It is true that Saul, the ardent persecutor of the church was a Pharisee (Acts 23:6) but he was converted and became the equally ardent apostle to the Gentiles. Furthermore, it was by appealing to the differences between Pharisees and Sadducees that Paul earns a temporary respite in his trial in Jerusalem (Acts 23:6–10). The Pharisees declared Paul innocent.

The popular image of the Pharisees is that they were religious snobs and hypocrites. In reality they were men who received a good deal of popular support. Josephus claims that

there were more than six thousand of them scattered throughout the kingdom in the time of Herod. At the same time Jerusalem may well have had a population of twenty-five to thirty
thousand. Their influence was amazing. They had complete
access to the king even though they refused to swear an oath to
loyalty to him. The chief sphere in which they exercised their
influence was, however, religious rather than political. Their
power was tolerated by the establishment simply because they
had popular support but, unfortunately for the establishment,
they often derived this mass support from the fact that they
were vociferous critics of the lay and priestly aristocracy.

Their religious aim was to build up the 'true Israel'. To do
so they voluntarily committed themselves to the rules of the
priesthood and they tried to bring practical piety within the
reach of the ordinary man. Jesus was appealing to the same
desires and needs in the ordinary people as the Pharisees were.
But his solution to their needs was very different. The Pharisees had succeeded only in laying a heavy weight of legislation
on people whereas Jesus offered a way of forgiveness and
freedom. It was this theological contrast which caused the conflict between Jesus and the Pharisees. It was this which ultimately led Jesus to his death.

Socially the Pharisees came from many different classes,
with perhaps the majority coming from the petty bourgeoisie.
As Jeremias says, 'Doubtless the Pharisees were the people's
party; they represented the common people as opposed to the
aristocracy on both religious and social matters.'[16] They would
then, to begin with, have much in common with the early
Christians. It was only as more and more non-Jewish elements
crept into the church that the differences between the Pharisees and the Christians became obvious and the rift between
them wide. For the same reason the early Christians lost the
support of the Jewish masses. They therefore placed themselves in a position where they might potentially come under
fire from new sources; the Pharisee party and the people (Acts
12:3 and 15:5).

The persecution of Stephen had its origins in the Synagogue
of the Freedmen (Acts 6:9). These Freedmen were Greek
speaking Jews who had once been slaves but now, together
with their families, had been given their freedom. It has been
suggested,[17] in the light of the information Luke gives about
these men, that they may well have been descendants of the
great number of prisoners of war taken by Pompey to Rome
where they had formed the greater part of the Jewish population. But that must remain a matter of speculation.

To have been a slave was in one sense no barrier to social advancement. Freedmen had found their way into the highest ranks of Roman society. Felix (Acts 23:24) is an example of how far a Freedman could rise in society if he wished to do so. Often Freedmen were used in high administrative positions and they would usually adopt the social status of their patron on being offered their freedom. Since, however, they were frequently despised by the aristocracy they would also often move away from Rome and they were to be found in many scattered places in the ancient world.

In spite of what has been said, the position of a Jewish Freedman was more difficult. For a Jew slavery was the very depth of social disgrace and disaster. Freedmen therefore were never easily accepted in Jewish society. Seen in this light the persecution of Stephen may well have been an opportunity for the despised Freedmen to ally with the regular Jews against a common enemy and so gain in prestige.

Just as the message of Jesus made most headway among those social groups who were longing for change so the message of his disciples was most readily accepted by and most clearly opposed by particular social groups. This is not to argue that there was any iron law of social determinism in operation in Jerusalem. Nonetheless, general patterns can be discerned. Those with vested interests in the preservation of the status quo were clearly opposed to the intrusion of this new group into their peaceful existence. Others saw the chance to oppose the new sect as chance to ingratiate themselves with the establishment and as a means of rising into the ranks of the socially accepted. Those with popular sympathies did not oppose the early Christians, until, that is, the Christians offended their own cherished ideas concerning racial or national purity. From then on the Christians were largely on thier own.

COGNITIVE DISSONANCE IN JERUSALEM

Sociology has also had something to say about the motives which drove the early disciples to seek to win converts so enthusiastically. The explanation, according to some sociologists, lies in the theory of cognitive dissonance. It is a theory developed by L. Festinger and others[18] and then taken up and applied more comprehensively, though with reservations, to the New Testament by John G. Gager.[19]

Put simply, the theory argues that when something we have

believed in is proved wrong, we feel a sense of discomfort or dissonance. To overcome that unease we could give up the belief. On the other hand there is another strategy we might employ. We might intensify our belief and persuade more and more people to share it. The idea is that if more and more people come to share our belief, it must, after all, be correct. Its popularity lessens our sense of discomfort.

Festinger has laid down five conditions if the dissonance is to lead to missionary activity.

1. The belief must be held as a deep conviction and have consequences in action.

2. The person must have taken some step which commits himself to the belief.

3. The belief must be specific and capable of specific disconfirmation.

4. The disconfirmation must occur and be seen to have occurred by the believers.

5. The believer must be in a group and the belief must be shared by others.

Others have subsequently qualified this point by saying that if it is shared by too many others, those whose belief is proved to be wrong will not need to proselytise since they will already have all the social support they require to go on believing.

Gager has added the comment that cognitive dissonance occurs primarily in new groups. Further, he argues that public ridicule can intensify missionary activity in the same way as when a belief is proved to be false. He also comments on the degree of disconfirmation which is possible before a person gives up believing. If the person is motivated by a real commitment to the truth of his belief, it may not be able to withstand much disconfirmation. More often, however, a person begins to believe because of his commitment to truth but continues to believe because of the satisfaction he gains from belonging to the group. When this happens his belief can withstand a greater amount of disconfirmation.

From one's own experience one can readily see a certain amount of truth in the theory. There is a stubborn streak in most men which makes it very difficult for them to admit that something they are committed to believing is wrong. Consequently even when the belief is patently wrong, they may still try to justify it or to make their position more comfortable by persuading others that they are right. There can be no doubt that there are some apparent believers in the church today who deep within them have doubts about the truth of the Christian faith. Rather than meeting these doubts and dealing with them properly, they engage in a frantic round of Christian activities in the hope that the doubt will be silenced.

The theory of cognitive dissonance has been applied to the New Testament in two ways. Its major application is to the church in Jerusalem. It is said that the Christians fully expected the imminent coming of the kingdom of God on earth. When the kingdom did not come, rather than forsaking their belief in Jesus as the Messiah, which it is argued had already been shaken once before by his unexpected execution, they engaged in intense missionary activity in an attempt to persuade others to believe too. All the five conditions which Festinger lays down are said to be detectable in this case.

In spite of this we need to ask if the theory really fits the Jerusalem church. Two issues in particular make its application in this instance questionable.

Firstly, the religion of Jesus Christ was from the very beginning a missionary religion. Missionary activity was not an afterthought but a basic and original ingredient of their faith (Lk. 9:1–6, 10:1–20; Matt. 28:19 and Jn. 20:21). In the light of this the early Christians are more appropriately seen in terms of being essentially a conversionist sect rather than as suffering from cognitive dissonance. It is true that there was a brief period of non-missionary activity between the crucifixion of Jesus and Pentecost but that was only a temporary interruption to their settled disposition as a missionary group.

Secondly, we must ask if the disciples really did expect the imminent setting up of the Kingdom of God on earth as the theory of cognitive dissonance, if it applies here, demands. During the lifetime of Jesus they clearly did have such an expectation (Matt. 20:20–22). However, as F. F. Bruce claims, 'the last flicker of their former burning expectation of an imminent political theocracy with themselves as its chief executives' is to be found as early as Acts 1:6.[20] It was not that what they expected to happen did not happen so causing them unease, rather it was that before it became a firm expectation, they learned that their expectation was wrong. In Christian terms they learned this not through a gradual realisation of their error but by a clear revelation from God at Pentecost. So they did not go on gaining support for a message which had been proved false, instead they preached the message that Jesus had been giving to them all the time, but which they had not fully understood. They were not, as Festinger's theory would seem to demand, gaining social support for a disconfirmed belief but for a belief which by definition is not capable of confirmation until the end of human history. Jesus had already told them that no one knew when his coming again was going to be (Mark. 13:32; Acts 1:7). The Christian belief in the imminent coming of the Kingdom of God is not that it will come soon so much as that it will come suddenly.

The missionary activity, then, of the early Christians was not so much to remove the discomfort of having made fools of themselves. That is a negative judgment which casts doubt on the validity of their belief. It was rather a positive affirmation of the good news that they now fully realised was availabe through Jesus.

The theory of cognitive dissonance is also applied by Gager to those converted to Jesus Christ. Here perhaps he is on firmer, if less developed ground. Paul is the classic example of someone whose conversion is a clear cut decision between two choices. The previous choice is rejected and the second choice decisively made. Paul, once an ardently religious Jew, now was converted into an equally ardent Christian whose missionary activities are well known. Why did he reject his old religious way so vigorously that things previously seen as an advantage were now seen as a liability (Phil. 3:4–11)?

Gager argues that the former religious views Paul held still had their attractions for him and so gave him a sense of unease about what he now believed. In order, therefore, to silence this discomfort, Paul, and others like him, strongly advocated the new faith they had acquired.

There is here an undoubted aspect of the truth for the simple reason that, as Gager points out, all new decisions involve some dissonance whilst important decisions related to the rejection of an attractive position may produce a great deal of dissonance. Even so it imputes rather negative motives to a man like Paul. Gager admits that the idea is somewhat undeveloped as yet and he further states that even if dissonance was a factor in the two issues mentioned in the New Testament church it is certainly not the whole explanation of their motivation for engaging in mission.[21]

The early church in Jerusalem may initially have been only a small and insignificant group but it was not a static group. Living as the early Christians did in a real flesh and blood world the Holy Spirit used the social networks of which they were a part to further the spread of the gospel. They ceased to be an introversionist Galilean sect and became instead an international conversionist sect. They moved forward because of the good news they had to share and because opposition forced them to. So the church began to take root in the very different soil of the Gentile world.

CHAPTER FIVE

The Gentile Environment and the Christian Gospel

Following the death of Stephen, Hellenistic members of the church in Jerusalem were forced to scatter. Wherever they went they took the good news of Jesus with them. Their activities seem to have caught the leaders of the Jerusalem church somewhat by surprise (Acts 8:14f, 11:19–24). For although they had already engaged in recruiting activity themselves among the Jews, it was quite some time before they realised fully the implications of the missionary commission which had been given to them. Peter was persuaded, with some difficulty, to engage in a little cross-cultural evangelism (Acts 10:1–11:18) and this resulted in the church discovering that 'to the Gentiles also God has granted repentance unto life' (Acts 11:18).

The real impetus for international missions came, however, not from Jerusalem but from Antioch. The church there was founded as a direct result of the persecution after Stephen's martyrdom (Acts 11:19–20) and from the beginning it seems to have possessed remarkable spiritual qualities (Acts 11:26). Judging from the names of its prophets and leaders (Acts 13:1) it is probable that there was also a culturally mixed congregation meeting in Antioch and this may well have accounted for the broad sweep of missionary vision which they had. It was from Antioch that Paul, the apostle of the Gentiles, was sent out to begin his work.

Although Paul initially preached to the Jews they did not respond warmly to his message. He found he was most welcome among the Gentiles. Since it is impossible to communicate to anyone in a total vacuum, and since effective communication inevitably means that the transmitter of the message is going to take into account the situation of his hearers, it is right to ask what sort of a world it was to which Paul preached and what effect it had on the shape of his message.

THE ENVIRONMENT OF THE ROMAN EMPIRE[1]

The foundations of the Roman Empire of the first century AD lie deep in history. The empire of Alexander the Great had disintegrated but not without leaving its mark on the language and the customs of the people. Rome preserved much of this culture even through weary years of civil war. Caesar and Pompey fought one of the last acts of that war which by their time had become a struggle for personal power. Caesar won, but was assassinated in 44 BC before he could build on his victory.

The new leaders Antony and Octavian divided the Empire between them, but that did not bring peace. Further discontent followed as men feared that Antony would transform Rome and the provinces into his personal toy like an oriental despot. There followed a chaotic struggle for power which Octavian won at the Battle of Actium in 31 BC. Octavian is said to have fought not for personal power but 'as a champion of Roman ideas, a champion of the Roman past and Roman future'.[2]

The years of struggle and unrest had filled the entire populace of the Empire with a yearning for peace. Octavian understood their longings well and was accepted as ruler just because he gave men the peace they wanted. The war, however, had altered the situation and the psychology of the people. Octavian theoretically restored the old form of government but he could not do so in practice. In reality power actually lay in his hands. The war had created an army which, though mostly stationed on the borders of the Empire, was loyal to its Commander-in-Chief, who was Octavian. He maintained the loyalty of the soldiers and their silence and citizenship at the end of their service.

Octavian renounced all special powers in 27 BC but was promptly given them back by the Senate. It was then that he took the name of Augustus. Further titles and honours followed. In 12 BC he became *pontifex maximus* and in 2 BC *pater patriae*. He was worshipped as a deity because he symbolised social stability. As Vergil put it,

This is the man,
This is the one whom you have long been promised,

Augustus Caesar,
Offspring of a god, founder of a golden age.[3]

Under Augustus the empire began to flourish. New roads and buildings proliferated and trade and commerce began to flow. Provinces maintained their independence and newly created territory was encouraged to adopt the form of the city-state. In this atmosphere the way was opened up for some to be upwardly socially mobile. Consequently there was an increase in the number of landowners and capitalists; many of whom had formerly been slaves. Augustus did not deliberately interfere with economics but his laissez-faire policies resulted in the disappearance of the peasantry and the gradual rise of industry and commerce. Augustus was more concerned to interfere socially in an attempt to reconstruct the old values of the Roman Republic. One of these values was the importance of family life which he attempted to rejuvenate by the adoption of various strategies including the issuing of a law making it illegal for an unmarried man to inherit property. In all these ways Augustus ushered in a new era and largely set the tone for the principal years of early Christian missionary activity.

Augustus died in 14 AD and was succeeded without opposition by Tiberius who ruled as Caesar throughout the period of the life of Jesus. He was a good and conscientious ruler who did much to consolidate the work of Augustus although after he went to live on Capri in 26 AD his relationship with the Senate suffered. He never visited them again and communicated with them through notes and messengers. After his death in 37 AD he was succeeded by Gaius who was also known as Caligula. Gaius thought the reign of Tiberius had been too solemn and he himself led a dissolute life. His early promise as a wise ruler was quickly dissipated and he was engaged in a series of disastrous campaigns on the eastern wing of the empire. His mental state began to deteriorate and he became a much more positive threat to the Christian church when he started to demand serious worship as a deity. Gaius was assassinated in 41 AD.

His successor, Claudius, is chiefly known for the administrative reforms he introduced and also for his expulsion of the Jews from Rome. He continued the policy of urbanisation, 'conscious that, once initiated into a civilised life, the (people) would be the best supporters of a regime which opened up to them important and wide opportunities.'[4] The policy of urbanisation led to economic growth in the provinces and consequently to the growth of the bourgeoisie. It also led to the concentration of wealth and land in the hands of the

Emperor. Slavery maintained its essential position in the empire. The chief social groups to suffer from the changes were, in fact, the old aristocratic families who were squeezed out by owners of ever larger estates and purged out by ever more powerful emperors.

Claudius was poisoned by his fourth wife, Agrippina, in 59 AD because she wanted to bring her son, Nero, to power. In the early days of his reign she exercised great influence over him but she was eventually replaced by other advisors. Nero's loyalty to Greek ideas and culture led to his unpopularity in Rome and in spite of some genuine achievements, under his control the political and economic affairs of the empire severely deteriorated. It is well known that he placed the blame for the fire of Rome on the Christians and they were sadistically persecuted as a result. Peter and Paul were probably both executed during Nero's time and it is against the background of his reign that some think the Book of Revelation was written. His savage dealings with the Christians was characteristic of his dealings with all his people and his sadism appears to have been part of his general disposition.

Nero took his own life in 68 AD and his death was the signal for the army to revolt. They had been responsible for the appointment of the last few emperors. Nero, however, had been indifferent to their affairs and so they chose the moment of his death to reassert their power. Civil war lasted for just over a year until Vespasian came to power and succeeded in re-establishing peace, strong government and economic order. During his reign arrangements were made for power to be transferred peacefully on his death to his son Titus. Sadly, although well-groomed for the office, Titus ruled only briefly (79–81 AD) before dying of fever. His brother, Domitian, who had been jealous of Titus's position followed him into power. Domitian extended the empire northward and strengthened the defence of the boundaries. But he will always be chiefly remembered as a tyrant who marked out the Christians for special persecution, including some in his own household. He was more fond of the title *Dominus et Deus* than any of his predecessors and naturally provoked opposition from the Christian church. He ruled until 96 AD when he fell victim to a conspiracy.

Against this political background a farily clear social hierarchy developed whose classes did not mix except in the performance of civil religion.[5] Its divisions had been sharpened into classes by Augustus. At the top of the hierarchy were the old Roman aristocratic families who composed the Senate.

Their position was based on heredity. By the time of Paul's missionary activities they were suffering from the economic and political changes which have been mentioned. One consequence of these changes was that the Senate opened its doors to many new members who came to Rome from the provinces and thus to some the purity of Rome was threatened.

Just below the Senate in legal rights and social dignity, but equal to them in wealth, was the Equestrian Order. They were part of the Establishment with the Senators but, since they were a powerful threat to the position of the Senators, they were resented by them. Usually such men would have a series of commands in the Army or the Fleet; held procurators' appointments; been in key positions in Rome or the Praetorian guard. The Emperor could add to this social rank without limit if the aspirants were free born and each had 400,000 sesterces to his name.

In the provinces many customary forms of local government were followed. Rome usually recognised these but even so two status groups at the upper end are usually distinguishable. Chiefly responsible to Rome would be the Council of the Decurians whose status was not all that dissimilar to the higher ranks of a County Council in our own time. A good job might be rewarded by acceptance into the Equestrian Order or at least the recognition of lesser rewards. On rare occasions it was later rewarded with a seat in the Senate. Immediately below the Decurians were the magistrates.

Towards the lower end of the social hierarchy there were three other groups. The free plebs were socially in the best position but were economically very vulnerable. Who would employ them when free labour was obtainable through slaves? Circumstances sometimes made it necessary for them to be given economic assistance by the Empire. Freedmen were formerly slaves who had been given their freedom by their master. Some were administrators but many served in quite ordinary jobs as sailors or firemen. At one stage the practice of setting men free became so common that it created something of a crisis for the Empire and Augustus enforced the regulations regarding manumission, as it was called, strictly.

At the very bottom came the slaves. They were throughout the period of the New Testament the backbone of the Empire. Most trade and industry was carried out by the slaves. A number of them were also educated and became the administrators for their masters. Prestige was somewhat governed by the number of slaves one owned and it is estimated that by the second century the Emperor possessed some 20,000 slaves.

The lot of the slave need not have been too bad, provided he was compliant with his master's will. At least he had some protection from the operation of naked economic forces. In addition it was possible for him to earn or win his freedom or to be adopted into his master's family.

THE RELIGIOUS ENVIRONMENT OF THE ROMAN EMPIRE

Christianity did not enter the stage of the Roman Empire as a solitary actor. The stage was already crowded with religions. First and foremost in the first century there was the growing worship of the Emperor. Augustus had not asked to be worshipped as a deity but nor had he objected to it when such worship was offered. Caligula and Nero openly courted such worship and by the time of Domitian the Emperor was unashamedly demanding it.

The worship of the Emperor was, to the Romans, not so much a spiritual matter as a civic duty. The Emperor symbolised the unity of the Empire and to worship him was to express one's political submission in the guise of religious ritual. For most men that was fair enough, as far as it went, but they also needed something more. They derived no personal or emotional satisfaction from such corporate worship of the state god. Augustus' policies had led to a growth in individualism and there were individual needs of a religious nature to be met as well, so many other gods and religious associations proliferated and were permitted to do so as long as they presented no political threat.

There were old Roman gods worshipped, at least in theory, by the higher social ranks. Like so many groups of establishment men, the Senators and Equestrian Orders were not given to much enthusiasm in religion and they probably believed in little. As the Senate was opened up to more and more members from the provinces so they grew to accept more and more gods from outside Rome. Whether such gods existed or not or whether dogma regarding them was correct or not was entirely unimportant. The crucial issue for them was whether it was useful to believe in such deities or not. A. D. Nock has summarised this religious attitude well. He writes:

> What did the ancients love? They loved local traditions and other traditions; which while alien in origin had become naturalised; they loved the worship of the household and of the state; they loved the reverent practices which had grown up around the dead.

What did they fear? The possible loss of benefits thought to be derived by State and individual from these inherited ways. What did they desire? Civic well-being; all the temporal blessings of this life; and the intangible things of which we have spoken—immortality sometimes, knowledge sometimes and a dignified status in the universe often. [6]

In the provinces a few who were aspiring to be noticed by Rome were zealous followers of the worship of the Emperor. But, for the most part, men really worshipped local deities. They may well also have belonged to one of the mystery religions which commonly provided emotional satisfaction. Mithraism is the best known mystery religion. It seems to have been particularly associated with the army and to have had no place at all for women. The various aspects of its worship were common to all such 'fellowships'. Great store was set on initiation ceremonies; in the case of Mithraism this was done in the blood of a bull. Members alone had the mysteries revealed to them. Fellowship was real in the sense that members of the cult saw each other as in partnership; joined in ceremonial meals and participated in mutual aid. There were, of course, cultic ceremonies to attend. In addition various forms of wonder-working may well have been practised. Resort to the supernatural was common in the ancient world but was usually an attempt to get the deities on your side. Perhaps only relatively rich men could actually become initiates into a mystery religion because it cost a sizeable sum of money to be initiated. In any case, the mystery religions had thousands of adherents.

Since Socrates, philosophy, too, had presented itself as a more popular alternative to religion. It was no longer reserved just for the professionals but wandering philosophers actively canvassed support for their explanation of the meaning of the universe. They even had their saints and their evangelistic literature. Perhaps, in the end, however, philosophy never quite touched the depths of an individual's need and so never became really popular.

It can now be understood why Christianity's entrance on to the Gentile religious stage was largely unhindered. Rome was officially indifferent to the multiplicity of religions and philosophies as long as they did not disturb the peace. If they did, Rome was always able to deal with them. To begin with the Christians were assumed to be a Jewish sect and since Judaism was permitted by the Empire nobody questioned the right of Christianity to exist. When, however, the distinction between Christianity and Judaism was drawn, Christianity became more vulnerable and its political liability was the subject of scrutiny. An illustration of this can be seen in the way in which the Jews tried to get Paul convicted of serious crimes. The Jews knew that there was no basis for conviction before a Roman court for any religious crime. So they framed their charge in political terms, that is, that Paul was 'a pestilent fellow, an agitator among all the Jews throughout the world' (Acts 24:5). The only limit that Rome set on the pluralism of religious belief was that it should not disturb the peace.

The religious environment of Rome was in some respects very similar to the religious environment of our own day.[7] On the one hand there was an established or generally accepted religion. On the other hand religion was, more realistically, a matter of private choice and personal opinion. The world was one of religious pluralism. The options open to a would-be believer were wide, although his choice was somewhat confined by his social situation or culture. Superficially it was much more of a supernatural world than our own. Though how much men seriously believed and how much they went along with, purely for reasons of social convention, we have no way of knowing. It could be that there was in fact widespread unbelief in a world populated so thickly with religion.

Into this pluralistic world came Christianity. Whilst it maintained the uniqueness of its message, it communicated it in such a way that many deliberately opted for it. However one might measure its success, one must agree that it made more than the expected amount of progress in the face of such diverse competition. What was it about the presentation of its message which appealed?

THE GOSPEL FOR THE GENTILE WORLD

In one sense the gospel preached by Paul to a Gentile world did not change at all from the gospel preached by Peter to a Jewish world. It still centred on Jesus of Nazareth in whom God had made known his love for men and his judgment of sin. It focused on his death, resurrection and coming again to rescue men from their sinful lives.

Yet the communication of the gospel changed when preached to the Gentiles. The language used was different, the arguments were varied and the models by which men could speak of God's love were suited to the Gentile context. In essence it had not changed, only in communication.[8] Without documenting the change fully, a number of illustrations can be given.

In the Gentile world Jesus was no longer spoken of as the long-promised Messiah but as Lord. The most common word for Lord in the New Testament is *kurios* which is used on 717 occasions. Of these, 485 occasions are to be found in the writings of Luke and Paul, that is, in writings written for 'people who lived in areas dominated by Greek culture and language'.[9] In the ordinary world *kurios* meant an employer or superior in contrast to a slave. The Hellenistic Jews had naturally used the term for God and Christians had applied it to Jesus. No doubt it was first applied to him out of politeness but its meaning became much deeper as they came to understand more of Jesus. In the end it became the basic Christian confession (1 Cor. 12:3). By the term they understood Jesus to be in a position of complete authority in the universe (Col. 1:10, 15–20) and of complete authority in the church, even to the extent of governing their ethical conduct (Rom. 14:8, 1 Cor. 6:13). The Lordship of Christ superseded all other master-slave relationships and so gave to them an entirely new character (Col. 3:22 – 4:1). To speak of Jesus as Lord was to state the truth in the form of a proposition. But it was also to conjure up in Gentile minds a whole image which was so common in their world and which could rapidly convey the essence of the believer's relationship to Christ.

Slavery too was another institution of the Roman Empire whose terminology was taken over and applied to a man's relationship with God. It is true that Jesus spoke in his parables about slaves. Even so it is Paul who develops the picture to its full extent. Before a person became a Christian he was a slave to sin (Rom. 6:15–23). When sin owned him he was the property not only of his fallen human nature but of Satan and he was destined for death. The work of Christ, however, was to set a man free. Freedom was one of Paul's great themes (Rom. 8:1–17; Gal. 5:1) and it was amply suited to his world. Many a slave longed for freedom from his human master and worked hard to earn it. Christ's work was a work of manumission given to men who could not possibly earn it. When a man had been set free he would usually adopt the status of his former master. The Christian convert too received a new status; the status of being Christ's man (2 Cor. 5:17). The Christian's freedom, however, is not a freedom which allows him to enjoy a selfish independence. It is curiously enough a freedom which bound him in a new form of slavery; a slavery to God (Rom. 6:15–23). This slavery paradoxically was a perfect form of liberty. In it a man learned to serve his Lord (Rom. 12:11; 4:18; Col. 3:24) and his fellow Christians (Gal. 5:13), not because he was forced to but out of voluntary submission. The crux of this paradox of slavery and freedom lay, for the Christian, in the fact that his master, the Lord of all, had himself voluntarily become a slave and taken upon himself the full consequences of being a slave to the extent of accepting the death penalty (Phil. 2:1–11). In this way not only was his lordship confirmed but he became an example to all believers.

A slave, when he was set free, did not always leave his master. He might well choose to remain a loyal servant of his master but working for him now as a member of the family rather than a slave. An ancient family would be very familiar with this and other forms of adoption. The importance for an ancient family of having sons can scarcely be over-estimated. It was not unusual for families, if disappointed in not having their own sons or if the sons they had disappointed them, to adopt sons. This image, too, Paul develops to his own ends and stresses both the present secure relationship a believer has with his Father God and the future inheritance which will one day be his (Rom. 8:22–24; Gal. 3:13–25; Eph. 1:5).

Changes took place not only in the way in which the essential core of the gospel was expressed but also in the ethical implications of that gospel. The same radical and conservative tension to which reference has already been made continues. The demands of believing the gospel are still radical without being totally destructive of the current social order. Many would argue that Paul was essentially conservative in his ethics, not concerned, except indirectly, with great changes in social structure, but this is a point to which we shall return. The essential point to note for the moment is that what Paul was doing was to apply the ethics of the gospel to a new social environment. Gone are the concerns of a Jewish religious society; uppermost now are the concerns of a pagan Gentile society. The dominant concerns therefore become those of moral and sexual ethics—(1 Cor. 5 & 6; especially 6:9–11; Eph. 4:28 etc.); family relationships (Eph. 5:21–6:4; Col. 3:18–21); relationships at work (Eph. 6:5-9; Col. 3:22–25) and attitudes to the state (Rom. 13:1–7; 1 Tim. 2:1–3). A further area which now becomes prominent is the topic of relationships within the Christian community itself (Gal. 6:1–6; Eph. 4:1–5:2; Col. 3:12-17).

Scholars have offered many different reasons for the success of the Christian message in the ancient world. Sociologically speaking, one overall reason for its success was that it suited the character and needs of the gentile environment so well. E. R. Dodds may be cited as one scholar who has perceptively identified four particular features of that suitability. Firstly, the exclusiveness of Christianity was a source of strength. In the midst of so many cults it made a clean sweep. 'It lifted the burden of freedom from the shoulders of the individual: one choice, one irrevocable choice and the road to salvation was clear.'[10] Secondly and paradoxically it was open to all. Thirdly, it held out to the disinherited a conditional promise of a better inheritance in another world. Other religions did too, but Dodds comments that 'Christianity wielded both a bigger stick and a juicier carrot.'[11] Lastly it offered benefits in the here and now. Christianity offered a new family and a deeper community life than other religions. It matched the needs of the pagan privatised Gentiles and so was attractive.

The transition then was made from the Jewish and rural environment in which the Jesus movement was founded to the Gentile and urban world of Rome. Jerusalem and the Jews are never lost sight of in the New Testament (Rom. 9:11). But they now share the stage with Gentile congregations in pagan cities whose sociological anatomy is different.

CHAPTER SIX

Roman Social Institutions and the Early Church

Man is inescapably a social being. According to the Bible he was designed from the beginning to live not in isolation but in relationship with others (Gen. 2:18). This gregarious aspect of man's nature needs channelling if it is to satisfy him rather than to leave him alienated and emotionally undernourished. It is neither possible nor wise for man to relate with the same degree of intimacy with every person he meets and so in order to satisfy his differing needs man creates or at least participates in social institutions of varying sorts. The most intimate of these is marriage and at the opposite end of the spectrum there is the international community.

The concern of this chapter is with three social institutions which, because they were current in New Testament times, are reflected in its writings. They are the city community (*politeia*); the household community (*oikonomia*) and the voluntary association (*koinonia*).[1] Each, at a different level, dealt with man's need to belong.

THE CITY COMMUNITY: *POLITEIA*

The republican institution of the city state flourished most under the Greeks. It was considered by them to be the best form by which an individual could associate with his fellow men. And were it ever to work ideally, they considered that it would result in utopia. Among its ideals were the full democratic participation of citizens in the city's affairs through the regular popular assembly. Public service was donated, voluntarily and enthusiastically, by the members of the city. Their willingness was secured by a healthy sense of competition which ensured that citizens remained highly motivated to participate in the city's affairs.

Long before the time of the New Testament the character of these city states had begun to alter. Man's belief in them still abounded and they had certainly not altogether disappeared. Yet the need for protection had forced the autonomous cities to seek strength through links with other city states. Eventually Rome became the overall protector and, although she encouraged much local freedom, her protection was bought only at the cost of subordination to her authority.

The relationship which a city state had with Rome was finely balanced. She might keep her own local rulers; issue her own coins;[2] perpetuate her own local customs and above all practise her own particular religion. It is against this background that the words of Jesus about the kings of the Gentiles have to be read (Luke 22:25) and the encounter between Herod and the people of Tyre and Sidon (Acts 12:19–23) has to be seen. The popular acclamation of Herod's divinity here stresses that religion was a central cohesive factor in these nation states. The people were always eager to claim that they had been privileged to be visited by a deity and prized the distinction that, such a claim involved by comparison with other city or nation states. Further illustrations of this can be found in reference to Paul's visit to Lystra (Acts 14:11–18); Ephesus (Acts 19:23–41) and Malta (Acts 28:1–6).

On the other hand the nation states enjoyed freedom only so long as they did not incur the displeasure of Rome. So their autonomy was, in fact, seriously compromised. The obligatory worship of the Emperor had been imposed upon the local religious cult and only the recalcitrant Jews successfully, if painfully, managed to resist it. In matters of law real power lay with Rome and the decisive factor, as the trials of both Jesus and Paul show (John 19:12 and Acts 25:23–27), lay with Caesar. Rulers, whether local or the envoys of Rome were aware that they would be maintained in office only so long as they governed efficiently and maintained peace.

The increasing centralisation of power in Rome enhanced the feeling of disenchantment men felt with this particular form of social institution. It was not until after the New Testament period that a complete sense of futility prevailed and a new fully-developed municipal system of government came into being. The dis-satisfaction, however, is reflected in the New Testament writings in three ways.

First, some men had already looked beyond the public life of the city or small nation to visions of a universal commonwealth or international brotherhood of man in which the divisions between men, which were so much a part of their experience, had been overcome.[3] The dream was too abstract to become very popular. Men need more personal structures of association than this concept could ever provide. Nonetheless the Christian Church presented itself as just such a universal brotherhood in which the common human barriers of culture, class, race and sex held no significance. All members of the church were one in Christ and 'brethren' in relation to each other (Romans 3:22–30; 10:12–13; 1 Cor. 10:17; 12:13; Gal. 3:26–28; Eph. 2:11–22; Col. 3:11).

Secondly, the church is compared to an ideal city and its members enjoy the rights and privileges of citizenship. It is a city free from all deficiencies which spoiled earthly attempts to find a perfect form of association in the *politeia*. (Eph. 2:19 and Phil. 3:20). The theme of the new city and the Christian's citizenship was to become even more prominent in post-Pauline writings (Heb. 12:22; 13:14 and Rev. 21).

Thirdly, the contrast between the church and the earthly city state must be pressed further. Ancient city or nation states were not fully egalitarian. For all their high ideals of democracy they functioned only because the privileges of membership were restricted. The high status and value of citizenship was preserved by excluding some from ever being able to acquire its status. Foreigners and slaves were two classes excluded by this ancient attempt at quality control. The church however consciously rejected this means of quality control. No discrimination was exercised on the basis of the usual social standards. All men could become members and citizens whatever their social, racial or national background and they all had an equal right to belong. The discrimination between member and non-member was made on the basis of faith in Christ—faith must be exercised if one wished to become a member (Gal. 3:2f). Other than this the New Testament writers go out of their way to emphasise that the Christian Church was for those who are 'foreigners', 'far-off' and 'aliens' (Eph. 2:12, 13 and 19); 'aliens' and 'strangers' (Heb. 11:13); 'strangers' (1 Pet. 1:1, 17) and 'aliens' and 'strangers' (1 Pet. 2:11).[4]

Apart from churches which consciously practise apartheid, discrimination in today's church is largely an unconscious matter. It sometimes takes a racial or nationalist form but more often, in the West, it is a matter of culture, class or background. Many of our churches operate unwittingly a respectability test and those who fail are subtly made unwelcome. Of course they are never told as much. It is just that they are patently not made as welcome as those with a socially respectable background. Perhaps every generation within the church needs to be aware of the insidious forms such worldly attitudes will take in order that the church might always be a great non-discriminating society.

THE HOUSEHOLD COMMUNITY: *OIKONOMIA*

The second social structure of the Roman world which demands attention is that of the household. It was both a fundamental institution of the New Testament world and of fundamental significance to the New Testament church. Failure to understand the household concept will mean that a good deal of the New Testament will remain at least a closed book if not a complete mystery. As Floyd V. Filson, who first drew attention to its significance in a seminal article, has said, 'The apostolic church can never be properly understood without constantly bearing in mind the contribution of the house church.'[5]

The Romans did not invent the household system, the Greeks had it too, but had subordinated it to the *politeia*. Under the Romans a number of economic and sociological changes took place which made the household the primary structure of the Empire. The old senatorial families of the republic declined whilst, at the same time, the increased distribution of wealth led to the founding of many more household communities. In addition to the extension in the number of households a further step elevated the importance of the structure. Augustus, needing to secure his authority, strengthened the personal links between himself and his servants and citizens. To do this he exploited the paternalism which was implicit in the household system and, using the emotional ties which it involved, he become the *pater familias* of the Empire. Consequently the empire became on a macrocosmic scale what the household was in microcosm. The empire was a complex network of households which all loyally interlocked into one grand system under the authority and protection of the Emperor.

What was a household community like? It was, in Hill's words, 'a large inclusive and socially cohesive unit'.[6] In a very real sense it was a community. It was composed of a number of families and sometimes, although unusually, individuals, who were bound together under the authority of the senior male of the principal family. They might well be engaged in a common agricultural or mercantile enterprise and live on the same estate. And there was no limit to the size of the household providing that the householder was able to support its members.

Its features were clearly delineated. There was a clear hierarchy of authority which culminated in the absolute power of the male head of the family. Under him the son, as the male heir, assumed a place of paramount importance. Where no such son existed, it was within the power of the father to adopt a son and make him his heir. The fact that adoption was both a familiar phenomenon in New Testament days and also a very valuable and treasured status is reflected in Paul's writings. It is one of the models he uses to describe the new relationship a person can have with God through Christ and in particular it is a model which emphasises the new status and both present and future privileges which will come to believers as a result of adoption (Rom. 8:12–25; 9:4; Gal. 3:26–4:7 and Eph. 1:5).

The household consisted also of friends and clients who might be freedmen or others whose association was valuable to the household. To be a friend or client was not to be the recipient of passing affection. For instance, a slave who was to be set free but who voluntarily chose to remain in a relationship with his master could enter into a new relationship which woud be binding. On the slave's part it guaranteed loyalty to the interests of the household and on the master's part it guaranteed provision for the material and social needs of the slave and his family. The new position is usually described as one of 'intimacy'. The master's affairs would become his affairs and they were in the joint enterprise together and without secrets. It was in this way that Augustus built up a system of friends bound by personal loyalty to him rather than to other seats of power in the Roman Empire. Judge has summarised this aspect of the household as follows:

> Friendship was not simply a spontaneous relationship of mutual affection. It was a status of intimacy conferred on trusted companions such as the associates of one's youth or else persons whose help was essential. Friendship conferred authority and prestige, the greater because undefined; it was from among friends that Caesar drew his principal advisers.[7]

This concept of friendship is also to be found in the New Testament. When Jesus told his disciples that they were no longer servants but friends (John 15:15) it was this meaning of friendship rather than our own looser sort he had in mind.

Likewise when Pilate was threatened at the trial of Jesus that if he were to release Jesus he would no longer be Caesar's friend (John 19:22), it was this very definite status that Pilate realised was at stake; not his vague acquaintance with the man at the top. Both these sayings allude to a common aspect of friendship, although they do so in a very different manner. Friendship involved loyalty and obedience. Disloyalty or disobedience could well result in the friendship being terminated.

The household was completed by the slaves who would be responsible for its day to day running, both in a practical and administrative sense. Their clearly defined status in the household would have provided them with security and perhaps even the eventual hope of freedom and friendship if they remained loyal and conscientious workers.

It can be seen that a household made up of the principal wealthy family, a number of friends and clients and a host of slaves was a thoroughly mixed community in terms of social status. Such a mixed community would need a powerful binding agent to keep its members united. Economic interests acted in part as the cement for friends and slaves. Slaves would additionally have faced legal sanctions if they had tried to break away. But over all these there was the morally binding force of religion. The solidarity of the household was expressed in the adoption of a common religion, chosen by the head of the house, which would serve not only to integrate them but to mark off their boundaries from others who worshipped different gods. Religion then served them in a classic Durkheimian way[8] in that it provided the means by which the collective soul of the family re-created itself and bound itself together.

This particular social institution is very apparent in the New Testament. Many of the parables of Jesus are set in a household of this extended kind, for example, the parables of the shrewd manager (Luke 16:1–13) and of the Talents (Luke 19:11–27). Furthermore Jesus is aware how crucial loyalty and unity were to such households (Luke 11:17). But it is in the Acts and epistles that the household becomes even more prominent.

Right from the beginning Christians met in the homes of some of their members (Acts 1:13; 2:46; 5:42; 12:12). The conversion and baptism of a number of households is also recorded, such as that of Cornelius (Acts 10:1–11:48); Lydia (Acts 16:13–15); the Philippian Jailer (Acts 16:31–34) and Crispus (Acts 18:8). From other parts of the New Testament we know of the conversion and baptism of other households as well, such as that of Stephanus (1 Cor. 1:16). later on it became the clear practice of the church to meet in the homes of its more wealthy members (Rom. 16:4, 5, 14, 15 and 23; 1 Cor. 16:19; Col. 4:15 and Phil. 2). The early church grew from a small local sect into a great international movement without the use of its own special buildings and with only the occasional resort to public buildings (e.g. Acts 19:9) of any kind.

The implications of the household structure for the early church were numerous and affected several different dimensions of their common life and mission. In Filson's article he identified five consequences of the household for the church. These will be listed first and subsequently other consequences will be added.

1. The household structure, centred on wealthy houses, enabled Christians to meet together for fellowship and worship right from their earliest days. They were not dependent on conforming to temple worship but were free to develop patterns which met their own needs and beliefs. Neither were they dependent upon building their own special buildings before regarding themselves as a true church. Archaeology suggests that some church buildings may have developed on the site of original house churches as the houses became too small to contain the number of worshippers.[9] But the use of public buildings in contrast to private houses did not develop on a widespread scale until the third century. In our own day when the health of the Christian religion is often wrongly measured, by sociologists and Christians alike, by the number of buildings set apart for exclusive Christian use, this may come as a shock to many. The importance of special buildings became grossly overemphasised in the mid-nineteenth century when, after the 1851 census, the number of church buildings was used as a pawn in the game of one-upmanship between Anglicans and Nonconformists. Many buildings, built even though there was no demand for them during that period, have become a gross liability to subsequent generations and a millstone which has hampered effective mission since.[10]

2. The importance of house churches partly explains why there is so much stress in New Testament ethics on family life and the master-slave relationships. Writing to house churches these would have been the areas of immediate concern to the new converts.

3. It is generally believed that the whole church in any one city rarely met together. Rom. 16:23; 1 Cor. 5:4, 14:23; 1 Thess 5:27; Heb. 10:25 and 13:24 are taken by some as implying that all the Christians in a city did not regularly meet

all in one place. In contrast the proliferation of meetings in people's houses indicates that there may well have been several different Christian groups meeting in various places in any one town. Although at first sight this seems to be placing a lot of weight on phrases like 'the whole church', 'all the brothers' and 'do not give up meeting together', such an explanation is probably right and certainly fits the context of the ancient world. Justin in his *First Apology* refers to several distinct house-based meetings in Rome as much as a century after the New Testament.

The point Filson makes at this juncture is that this fragmented structure explains the tendency to party strife in a place like Corinth. As birds of a feather flock together, so Christians with certain emphases or tendencies were likely to congregate around certain households. Maybe their respective fan clubs would be based on the houses in which Paul, Cephas or Apollos had stayed whilst visiting Corinth.

Two further things can be said about this. Firstly, no structure is without blemish or, to express it in other words, no one structure is specifically Christian. Some structures may be more useful or amenable to the Christian faith than others but all need to be treated with discernment in case unfortunate side effects occur. Secondly, no one small group can claim to be the whole church of God. Paul refrains from calling the house groups the church of God[11] and does so only as they all assemble together in one place. The church must always be a widely-embracing and diverse group of believers and never just the groups of people whose company, or expression of faith one personally happens to find congenial.

4. The household structure also illuminates the vexed question of the social status of the early Christians. This issue will receive a detailed examination in the next chapter, but Filson's conclusion may be stated as an anticipation of the conclusions which will be reached there. The apostolic church was a cross-section of society reflecting the social mixture which would have been found in any household community—from wealthy landowner to common slave.

5. Finally, Filson mentions the implications of this structure for the leadership of the Church. The hosts of the church which met in their house would inevitably become the leaders of the church. They were undoubtedly men of wealth, education and ability and as Gentile 'God-fearers' they had already showed themselves people of some independent thought. So they had also proved themselves to be people of initiative and decision. We actually know the names of many such people in

the New Testament and will refer to them again in the next chapter. The suggestion, however, must not be taken too far for the leadership of the Christian Church was not exclusively confined to those qualified on social grounds but to those spiritually qualified, even if they were less qualified on other grounds. A further detail which Filson adds at this point is worthy of note. The house churches were eminently suited to the training of future leadership which would provide the church with guidance in post-apostolic days.

To these implications a number of others may be added.

6. Conversion in the New Testament was not always an exclusively individual act. It was often a decision taken by the whole household. Reference was made earlier to the conversion of Cornelius, Lydia, the Philippian Jailer, Crispus and Stephanus, together with their households. In the context of our western individualism it is hard to grasp how any decision can be a genuine and personal decision unless individually taken. Yet in other social contexts people do not see the strong divorce we make between the individual and the corporate.[12] Thus a decision can be authentically personal, and an individual can be very much a party to the decision, whilst the decision is taken by someone else.

So it was in the matter of religion in the New Testament world. A household, as we have seen, expressed its solidarity through its adoption of a common religion. The religion would be that one chosen and practised by the *pater familias*. He was the key decision-maker regarding any decision, religion included. The result was that if he decided to become a Christian, his household would genuinely follow him. Concern need not be expressed therefore in regard to the household baptisms, as it has been expressed in the past, as to whether it was proper to baptize other members of the household, including possibly children, who may themselves not have taken individual decisions to follow Jesus Christ. For in such matters corporate multi-personal decisions were taken by the householder and accepted by the rest of the household.

The application for today[13] in a much more individualistic culture is not that we should consider it inherently wrong to take individual decisions. It is that our evangelism should still be aimed at the decision makers in our community and families. Even with our advanced state of individualism we still have decision-makers who significantly affect others. In many cases, despite all the advanced opinions propagated through the media, it is still the father of the family or, at least, the parents jointly. How wrong then that much of today's evanglism is directed towards the children who do not, generally speaking, have the power to influence those who are still making major decisions for them.

7. As an extension of the last point we may note how Paul uses the household in his missionary strategy.[14] During his first missionary journey Paul had to use the synagogues as a base for his evangelism. Whilst not ignoring these it is true that he subsequently aimed at the conversion of a household which could form the nucleus of the church he hoped to found. The household gave him not only a good number of converts initially but probably a centre for his future operations. All this is clear in the cases of Lydia and Stephanas. A household was well suited to serve as a centre for evangelism to other households and the surrounding neighbourhood in general. This would occur, not least, through the day-to-day contacts the household would have with others for business or commercial reasons. Indeed it may be that the adoption of this new strategy was essential if Paul was to make any impression with a new religion in unfamiliar territory.

8. A final implication concerns the role of minority groups in the ancient world and in particular the place of women. Christianity gave both women and slaves a new status and a new opportunity to participate fully in religious activity. There was no theological barrier to their full participation (Gal. 3:28 and Col. 3:11). Even so the basing of Christian worship on the household facilitated the practice of their participation in the church.

Judaism left women religiously uneducated; treated them as of no significance in the meeting of a synagogue for which ten men had to be present; and made them leave their segregated worship before the teaching of the law. In the mystery cults their participation was limited. Some cults, e.g. Mithraism, were rigidly male preserves whilst even those, such as Isis, which gave them a role as priestesses, were practised more by men than women. The case of Lydia (Acts 16:13–15) demonstrates the crucial part played by women in the founding of the church. Romans 16 convincingly shows that Paul could not have carried on his missionary activity without them and that he gives to some, e.g. Phoebe (v. 1), the highest honours. 1 Cor. 11 describes their participation in worship, given certain conditions, including the use of the gift of prophecy (v. 5) which Paul later places among the chief gifts (1 Cor. 12:28). Only the position of full-blown authority is denied them (1 Tim. 2:11–15).

Slaves were also in a position to participate fully alongside their masters in Christianity for they were given an equal status with them before God. In Judaism they were despised, whilst in the mystery religions, although they sometimes had theoretical freedom to participate, the cost of initiation was usually enough to make sure that few did so. Christianity, however, had no such financially prohibitive factor and so participation with full dignity was not only permitted but possible.

The exposition of the household concept leads one to agree with Filson and other scholars who have subsequently seen it as of fundamental importance in the early church. It may not have provided Paul with his most significant theological model for the church, which was the church as a body, but it was a sociological model whose ramifications were everywhere to be seen.

THE VOLUNTARY ASSOCIATION: *KOINONIA*

Many members of the Roman Empire were able to find security in either the city state or household community. Security often arises from having a definite place in society and also a personal identity. The household was especially well adapted for these purposes. Even so it did not provide for all the needs of the individual and as time went on a new form of association developed. In these voluntary and unofficial associations people's deeper and emotional needs were met. We have many such groups still in our own day whose chief function, as distinct sometimes from their declared aim, is to provide followship.

Voluntary associations proliferated, especially in Greek areas, in New Testament days. Many of them would be quite small but that was essential if they were to provide the depth of personal relationship which was required. People would gather with a common interest; a social or philanthropic cause; a trade or philosophy. Some associations were explicitly religious but all of them, irrespective of their *raison d'être*, would have had a religious dimension built into their activities.

Emotional satisfaction was catered for in a number of ways by these associations, not simply by the sense of belonging to a small group to which we have already referred. To opt for membership of an association was a deliberate and conscious act which marked you off from your fellow men. It gave you a sense of knowing something, a sense of status, your neighbour did not have. Many of the activities of the association were a mystery to non-members and it is always an emotional fillip for a man to believe he is in the know when others are not. For the most part Rome expressed little concern about these associations. But their exclusiveness and secrecy was a potentially worrying fact for the government. Occasionally, therefore, Rome would stir from its official lack of concern and ban an association if it considered its meetings a threat to security. The Jewish population would form just such an association in many cities of the Empire and an example of the unease Rome sometimes felt about their activities is seen in expulsion of the Jews from Rome under Claudius referred to in Acts 18:2.

The activities of the association catered also for man's emotional needs. Entry into the association would be marked by an initiation ceremony. It might well consist of a ritual bath or other purification rite. It might be preceded by fasting and have the character of a secret ceremony about it. The parallels to Christian baptism at first sight seem obvious. Christianity changed such initiations however not only in the content and meaning which it attributed to them but also in that it democratised them. Initiation into a mystery cult or voluntary association was theoretically open to all.[15] The sociological function of initiation was always the same, no matter what its precise form or meaning. It acted as a very tangible boundary which separated the initiate from his previous life and from the lives of his fellows who were uninitiated. It therefore enabled the initiate to be conscious of his new status and was a crucial stage in the process by which an interested enquirer would become committed to his new companions.

Other activities provided the emotional outlet and the means of social support which the member would seek. Frequent meals would be held and worship would be offered to the association's deity (see 1 Cor. 8). Mysteries would be made known to the initiates. Even miracles would be worked as a vindication of the deity who was worshipped. But for the most part the associations acted, not as religious bodies, but as ancient friendly societies caring for members during sickness and especially concerned to provide for the eventual expenses which would be incurred at one's funeral. They were places of brotherhood.

Judaism was perceived as one of these voluntary associations by the Roman Empire. It was an association with a difference, however, in that despite its rigid exclusivism it was international in scope and anything but small in scale. It is not surprising that when Christianity was born it made headway in the world because it came under the umbrella of Judaism (e.g. Acts 26:2–3). No one therefore noticed its separate existence and even when questions were raised in the minds of Roman officials there was little need for concern because it was seen to be yet another voluntary association. Only when it threatened the peace of the Empire did it receive detailed examination.

Confirmation that Rome viewed Christianity in this light is to be found in a letter written to the Emperor Trajan in c. AD 112 by Pliny, who was responsible for the government of Bithynia. He was at a loss to know what to do with the Christians against whom many accusations had been made and who were rapidly growing in numbers. Pliny examined some who confessed to be Christians and wrote to Trajan,

> They maintained, however, that the amount of their fault and error had been this, that it was their habit on a fixed day to assemble before daylight and recite by turns a form of words to Christ as a god; and that they bound themselves with an oath, not for any crime, but not to commit theft or robbery or adultery, not to break their word, and not to deny a deposit when demanded. After this was done, their custom was to depart, and to meet again to take food, but ordinary and harmless food; and even this (they said) they had given up doing after the issue of my edict, by which in accordance with your commands I had forbidden the existence of clubs.[16]

The compliance of the Christians with the ban shows how alert they were to their precarious status as a voluntary association. These Christians were willing to forego the advantages of short-term association in order to prevent their total extinction by the power of Rome. To be under such a ban was not an uncommon state of affairs. Many voluntary groups had experienced the same and had also learned the way in which, given time, the grip of Rome would be relaxed; allowing them to meet again.

The genius of early Christianity lay partly in its ability to present itself as an ideal form of the social structures which already existed in the Roman Empire. Men discovered that they were able to relate to their fellow men on all three of the levels they felt they needed. On the grandest scale they became, through the church, citizens of an international and totally new city. They knew also the security of a well-defined place which they enjoyed in the household order. Neither of these prevented them from entering into the warm and personal relationships which were characteristic of the voluntary clubs and associations. The offer of significant relationships on each of these levels was one of the most attractive features of the early church.

Recently, students of church growth have spoken of the need for churches to offer people the opportunity to relate to others through different-sized groups.[17] They have identified that three groups are necessary to meet man's various needs as he joins with his fellow men. Each group operates in a totally different way because it is governed by different principles of group dynamics, according to its size. The largest group meets for *celebration*. It focuses on inspiration and worship and it uplifts the individual even though he can be anonymous within it. Then there is the *congregation* which is a smaller unit, maybe of about 100, although various figures are quoted, where people know each other and can recognise strangers. Its functions are education and involvement in the many tasks of mission which are the responsibility of a church. It also begins to provide for the needs of personal fellowship. But it is the third level, the *cell*, which really provides for in-depth personal fellowship. Here a small group of people can become thoroughly acquainted with each other and support each other through sharing in Bible study and prayer.

The parallels between these structures, recommended in our own day, and those of the early church are not exact and should not be forced. Yet there is a similarity between the two sets of groups and their functions. When the whole church met together in an ancient town or area it probably became conscious of being part of an even-greater body of people. It would have found such meetings as inspiring as the celebration events spoken of by today's church growth scholars. A congregation has certain similarities to the household, whilst the cell provides the same depth of relationship as the voluntary association.

There is then an indication that the church today must take seriously man's need to associate with others and must provide structures which will enable him to do so in various ways according to his several needs. The details and forms of the structures today will rightly differ from those in the early church. It is not possible to duplicate them nor would they suit our industrialised world if we could. But we ought to have the same insight into patterns of association as the early church did in its own day for they can either hinder or enable growth both for the individual person and the church as a whole. Because man is a social being these structures inevitably have a significance which cannot be avoided and should not be ignored.

CHAPTER SEVEN

The Social Status of the Early Christians

The concept of social class is fundamental to modern sociology. It is used as an analytic tool to describe contemporary
society and is also central to any explanation of how societies
change. Social classes in the ancient world were obviously very
different from those of our own world and the concept must be
used in reference to the New Testament with care. Nonetheless a farily rigid social hierarchy did exist in the ancient world
and its divisions had been reinforced by Augustus as part of his
policy of reconstructing the Empire. The basis of the class system was birth and legal status rather than wealth. A senator
might not be very rich but he was at the top of the social hierarchy and was secure in his status.[1]

A discussion of the social classes represented in the New
Testament is important for a number of reasons. To begin
with a number of popular images exist which are not necessarily borne out by the facts. Secondly, these popular images
are sometimes used for ideological purposes to the detriment
of contemporary Christianity. Thirdly, it is often said that
Christianity was originally a religion of the oppressed or
deprived who adopted an ethic of poverty but that this ethic
was reinterpreted, if not abandoned altogether, as Christianity
gradually attracted more wealthy and prestigious people to its
ranks.

The popular image of Christianity owes much to Paul's comment that, 'not many of you were wise according to worldly standards, not many were powerful, not many were of noble birth;
but God chose what is foolish in the world to shame the wise, God
chose what is weak in the world to shame the strong, God chose
what is low and despised in the world, even things which are not,
to bring to nothing things that are...' (1 Cor. 1:26–28).

Many have taken Paul's statement at face value, not even allowing any qualification in the light of Paul's rhetorical argument in the opening of his letter to the Corinthians, and made the general assumption that therefore early Christianity was a lower class phenomenon. Frederick Engels gave the classic Marxist formulation of this view when he wrote:

> The history of early Christianity has notable points of resemblance with the modern working class movement. Like the latter, Christianity was originally a movement of oppressed people; it first appeared as the religion of slaves and emancipated slaves, of poor people deprived of all rights, of people subjugated or dispersed by Rome.[2]

This position was further developed by other influential Marxist writers, most notably Karl Kautsky. He cites as evidence for his views both 1 Cor. 1:26 and Jerome who said that Christianity recruited not from the Lyceum or the Academy but from the lowest rabble. In fact, Kautsky claims, it was a common joke in the Roman Empire that Christians could convert only the simple minded. So, without hesitation. Kautsky adopts as his hypothesis that,

> Christianity in its beginnings was without doubt a movement of impoverished classes of the most varied kinds, which may be named by the common term 'proletarians', providing this expression be understood as meaning not only wage-workers.

And,

> It is generally recognised that the Christian congregation originally embraced proletariat elements almost exclusively and was a proletarian organisation. And this was true for a long time after the earliest beginnings.[3]

Kautsky finds further support for his views in the 'savage class hatred' which the New Testament demonstrates towards the rich and in the communistic organisation of the primitive Christians.

The description of the early Christians is not for Kautsky an end in itself; it is a means to an end. The point is to prove that the history of Christianity is the history of one long betrayal of its origins. Originally it had given the proletarians hope of freedom but instead of fulfilling its promise, it had been transformed into one more tool with which the establishment might oppress the poor. In Kautsky's own words,

What the Jews had vainly hoped for from their Messiah of royal lineage was accomplished by a crucified Messiah, who had issued forth from the proletariat: he subjected Rome, he brought the Caesars to their knees, he conquered the world. But he did not conquer the world for the proletariat. In its victorious course, the proletarian, communistic beneficial organisation became transformed into the most tremendous instrument of domination and exploitation in the world.[4]

For very different reasons Ernst Troeltsch similarly argues that the early Church was populated by the poor and oppressed and that the wealthier people did not enter it until the second century. Troeltsch's point is that the early church developed as a result of its spiritual energy and not because any favourable social dynamic was in operation. Even Paul, whom some might regard as responsible for corrupting an otherwise simple faith for simple people, Troeltsch described as:

. . . an unliterary person in an unliterary class of the Imperial period but as a spiritually gifted man he rose out of his class and regarded the surrounding world of contemporary culture with a supreme sense of power. All his scattered attempts at systematisation reveal the limitations of his powers; the secret of his greatness lay in the realm of formless religion.[5]

A New Testament theologian, Adolf Deissmann, too argued that the adherents of early Christianity were of very low social status. His justification for this position lay in the low level of literary culture which the New Testament displays judged in its contemporary Greek context.[6]

The image, then, of the early church as a movement of the poor and deprived has been well established and generally accepted. Today, it is frequently used by those who still believe in it to induce guilt in the members of the predominantly middle class western church. But how accurate is it? Recent scholarship has tended to present a different picture.

The question can be answered only by a fairly detailed examination of the status of the people who are mentioned in the New Testament. The focus of this chapter will be on Paul and his churches, since reference to the socio-economic position of the followers of Jesus has already been made.

Even before Paul's ministry there are indications of wealthy and middle class people in the church. Barnabas clearly had some wealth (Acts 4:37) and Cornelius was hardly a member of the proletariat (Acts 10:1). Judea may not have been the most attractive part of the Empire in which a soldier could be stationed, but even so, as a Roman Centurion based in prosperous Caesarea, Cornelius must have been a member of the middle class. With Paul's conversion and ministry, the class basis of the early church became even wider.

THE APOSTLE PAUL

It is not possible to locate the apostle Paul himself with any degree of exactitude in the social system but a number of factors combine to cause one to reject Troeltsch's estimate of him and to place him solidly in the middle class and possibly in the upper middle class.

It cannot be said for certain but it is possible that Paul received a rhetorical education at Tarsus. Rom. 1:14 may be an allusion to this and his facility to speak with confidence at the Areopagus a further indication of it. Paul himself stressed the education he received from Gamaliel (Acts 22:3). Whether we view Paul simply as trained as a Rabbi or trained in addition as a sophist,[7] his education was an elite and expensive one.

Tarsus, as Paul himself said, was no mean city. It had long enjoyed the favours of Roman Emperors. Under Augustus it was exempted from imperial taxation and Augustus further settled his former tutor, Athenodorus, there as administrator. It was the ancient equivalent of a university city; a centre of culture and learning. To be a citizen of Tarsus one had to pass the means test of owning property worth 500 drachmae. Paul and his family must have fulfilled this qualification.

The reason for Paul's family being granted Roman citizenship is unknown. It could be that his father or grandfather had rendered some special service for the Emperor or other high official, perhaps in connection with their tent-making business. But any such view is mere speculation. The status, however, guaranteed for Paul certain rights and privileges above the normal level that a member of the empire could expect. Originally the status had been granted only to free-born citizens of the city of Rome but its privileges were made more widely available as the borders of the empire extended. For Paul and others it was a prized possession which proved useful to him on more than one occasion (e.g., Acts 16:37 and 22:25 ff).[8] It put him among the social elite of the empire.

Paul was a typical product of Tarsus. He was at home in the cultured Greek world and fluent in several languages; but he was also at home as a citizen of Rome. These aspects of his heredity and environment combined with his Jewish back-ground to make him uniquely gifted as a missionary to the Gentiles on behalf of a Jewish Messiah.

There are other indications of his fairly high class position. In Jerusalem he had easy access to the high priest (Acts 9:1f) and volunteered to head a persecution campaign against the Christians. His attitudes too, as Hill has pointed out, are those of someone from the upper middle class. Suffering does not come easily to him. On the contrary, accepting deprivation and pain was a lesson Paul had to learn through hard experience (Phil. 4:11–13). His attitude to work is that of a middle class person (Eph. 5:5–8; Col. 3:22-25; 2 Thess. 3:10, 11). The difference between Paul's and other middle class views of work is that Paul transforms work from being a mere duty into being a duty towards God. His whole approach to work relationships and other social ethical issues betrays a slight social conservatism which one would equate most naturally with a person whose background was that of the upper middle class. Hill has also seen this attitude come through in his relationship with the churches he founded where he 'displays all the arrogance of an aristocrat in dealing with his recalcitrant followers while at the same time reflecting the typical attitudes of the establishment towards all existing social institutions.'[9]

Paul's willingness to adopt manual labour as a means of support is no obstacle to the view of his fairly high social class origins. Manual labour was regarded highly by the Jews and treated with dignity. It was not despised but was rather accepted as the normal means of training and support.

It would seem that Troeltsch's judgment of Paul is ill-founded and that, instead of being an 'unliterary man', Paul was educationally and socially of a more than average standard.

PAUL'S CONVERTS AND SUPPORTERS

A careful look at those who became Paul's converts or sponsors demonstrates that the Christian church from the very beginning was socially mixed. It was no homogeneously proletarian movement.

Paul's first missionary journey began with the conversion of the Proconsul of Cyprus (Acts 13:12). From then on, however, Paul seems to have run into one set of opposition after another. Often it was the Jews combined with establishment figures who took steps to remove Paul from their boundaries, as can be seen at Antioch (Acts 13:50); at Iconium (Acts 14:5) and at Lystra (Acts 14:19).[10]

E. A. Judge has argued that between Paul's first and second missionary journeys Paul consciously changed his strategy.[11] On the first journey his platform had been the Jewish synagogue and, as a result, he encountered much opposition. Nowhere on that journey do we read of him claiming his Roman citizenship or in any other way attempting to counter the opposition. On his second and third journeys Paul created an alternative platform for his preaching. He used his status as a Roman citizen and often managed to acquire influential sponsors to support him. The Jews and the populace were still frequently hostile but Paul had broken the alliance between Jews and the Gentile establishment which had cost him dear on his first journey.

Judge sees the turning point in Paul's strategy as coming at Philippi (Acts 16:11–40). Here, for the first time, a wealthy patron is introduced and Paul also protests about the illegal treatment he had received as a Roman citizen. Lydia is the first of about forty people who can be identified as Paul's supporters, or would-be supporters if the occasion arose. She was clearly wealthy since she was an importer of luxury textiles from Asia and apparently had a large house (Acts 16:14–15). At Thessalonica it was the lower classes which again turned against Paul whilst Jason, who was wealthy enough to put down money for security, and the leading women supported him (Acts 17:9, 4). At Berea Paul again found his response among 'a few Greek women of high standing as well as men' (Acts 17:12).

Paul's visit to Athens took him to the intellectual elite of the Empire where he seems to have been able to speak to them from their own philosophical foundations without difficulty (Acts 17:16–34). One convert, Dionysius, belonged to this intellectual elite whilst a woman, Damaris, is mentioned, who, it is fair to assume, would have been a woman of some social standing.

Corinth will be temporarily passed over so that it can be examined in more detail later in the chapter. At Ephesus Paul's mission is organised in a manner similar to that of a middle class operation and quite unlike that of a proletariat movement. A hall is hired and regular teaching is given over a period of three years. Paul's work was so successful that many became followers of Christ, with the result that the economic basis of the town was threatened. The situation provoked a public demonstration which is illuminating in that it further shows how acceptable the preaching of Paul had become to the town authorities. Paul's associates, Gaius and Aristarchus, are obviously well known and Luke explicitly says that Paul could name the Asiarchs among his friends. The Asiarchs were leading citizens who came from the noblest and richest families and whose civic duties wer religious rather than political in nature (Acts 19:31). The town clerk deprecated the manner in which Demetrius and his colleagues had expressed their complaint against Paul and argued that proper legal channels were open to them should they wish to protest further.

The picture presented thus far shows that the Christian message appealed to a number of the members of the middle class as well as to those in the working classes. But it could be that the picture has been deliberately painted in this way, since it is commonly thought that part of Luke's purpose in writing the Acts is to demonstrate to the Roman authorities how acceptable and politically unsubversive the preaching of Christ was. If that was his purpose, it would be natural for him to emphasise the status and wealth of the converts at the expense of the common followers.

One possible check on Luke's portrait in Acts is to look at other parts of the New Testament where the self-conscious defence of the faith before the establishment is not a factor. In this regard Romans 16 becomes important. The Epistle to the Romans is itself a highly complex theological argument which is unlikely to have been addressed to a solidly propetarian congregation. Shirley Jackson Case used that point some years ago to argue that Rome represented a class of Christian people who were above the status of those Paul was used to dealing with. They were, Case said, people who felt that Paul needed to be steadied by tradition and the law and who thought Paul was too liberal in his attitude to the Jews and the Old Testament.[12] But there seems no good reason for the suggestion that, in the light of these theological issues, Paul and his readers at Rome represented two different class views of Christianity. In fact, the evidence of Romans 16, assuming it to be genuine,[13] is that Paul was quite at home with many members of the church at Rome.

In Romans 16 Paul names several of his patrons and fellow-workers. The list is tantalisingly brief but even so some people can be ascribed their social location with a fair degree of probability. Phoebe (v. 1) is a Gentile name derived from pagan mythology and was probably a freedwoman. She was able to offer assistance to many. Priscilla and Aquila (v. 3) are frequently mentioned with gratitude by Paul. Aquila we know to be a Jew and a tent maker (Acts 18:2) who was expelled from

Rome, probably as part of a general expulsion of Jews by Claudius, and who eventually hosted a church in his house at Ephesus (1 Cor. 16:19) before returning to Rome. Some have thought that the placing of Priscilla's name before that of her husband indicates that she was an aristocratic Roman lady but the suggestion, whilst not impossible, is based on slender evidence. Their mobility and ability to host a church fellowship, together with their hospitality to Paul, does suggest some wealth.

Little is known of some of the people mentioned in the list even though Paul regards them highly. Epaenetus (v. 5), Mary (v. 6), Tryphena (v. 12), Tryphosa (v. 12) and Persis (v. 12) are among these little-known individuals. Some names are common slave names such as Ampliatus (v. 8), Phlegon (v. 14), Hermes (v. 14) and Philologus (v. 15), whilst others appear among the names of members of the Imperial house, e.g. Apelles (v. 10).

For our purposes two names are of particular interest: Aristobulus (v. 10) and Narcissus (v. 11). It is quite likely that Aristobulus was the grandson of Herod the Great and brother of Agrippa I. He himself was not greeted by Paul, possibly because he himself was not a Christian, but members of his family were sent warm greetings as fellow-believers. Similarly it was the family of Narcissus, rather than Narcissus himself, who were greeted. It is usually thought that this Narcissus was the famous and very wealthy freedman of the Emperor Claudius whom Juvenal mentions and who exercised tremendous influence over Claudius. The fact that he personally was not greeted either implies that he was already dead or that he had not himself become a Christian.

The significance of the list then is to indicate that a thorough social mix had taken place in the Roman church. By no means can it be claimed that this church was exclusively a lower class group since it definitely contained a number of wealthy and influential people and probably included a number who were well-connected through their families, even to the imperial house itself.

In rejecting the popular view of early Christianity as a lower class movement caution must be exercised lest the pendulum swing too far in the opposite direction. It is not right to argue that, rather than being working class in character, early Christianity was a middle class movement. Some of the names examined may give that impression but, sadly, the writing of history repeatedly suffers from the fact that it is usually the important or the articulate whose names and deeds get recorded. To some extent this tendency is evident in the New Testament as well, although, as Romans 16 shows, it is not completely true of these writings. It must always be remembered that behind the people whose names are recorded there was a host of unnamed individuals, many of whom we know from other sources to have been members of the great mass of common people. The most appropriate conclusion about the early Christians is therefore that they represented all social classes except the aristocratic class and that the church reflected the diverse social classes to be found in the wider society. The conclusion should come as no surprise, for it is exactly what one would expect if the analysis of the significance of the household in the previous chapter was correct.

A CASE STUDY: CORINTH

A knowledge of the social class background of the early Christians is not only interesting in its own right but often holds the key to understanding problems to be found within the early church. Corinth is a case in point. No church in the early days of Christianity seems to have suffered so many problems as this church.

Theologians have for some time probed the First Epistle to the Corinthians in order to help them diagnose what the root cause of their difficulties were. Some have found signs of an incipient Gnosticism, whilst more recently many have put down the cause to the Corinthians holding an over-realised view of eschatology.[14] No one would wish to dispute the presence of such doctrinal errors nor that doctrinal error can have a disruptive effect in terms of social relationships. It has long been accepted within sociology, thanks to the work of Max Weber, that ideas do play a role in shaping people's behaviour. The apostle Paul, too, believed that correct behaviour arose from correct belief and faulty behaviour often had its origin in faulty belief. On the other hand the theories of some theologians give the impression that the early Christians were not ordinary people but budding intellectuals whose major preoccupation was a discussion of academic and abstract theology. Surely this was not the case. Perhaps therefore the theories about the theological problems at Corinth need to be coupled with an understanding of ordinary social relationships and the problems that occur within them, even inside the church.

Looking at the social composition of Corinth we find, as we did at Rome, that it was not a socially homogeneous church. Paul's statement in 1 Cor. 1:26 is partly made for rhetorical effect but, even so, it must have some basis in reality and there must have been many members of the Corinthian church who were slaves or belonged to the common people. Yet we also know that the church contained some wealthier people.[15]

Priscilla and Aquila were associated with Corinth. Other people who are named include Crispus (1 Cor. 1:14) who was the ruler of the synagogue and rulers were usually rich men (Acts 18:8) and Gaius whom some think to be the same person as Justus (Acts 18:7). Romans 16:23 speaks of Gaius as Paul's personal host and the host to the whole church, thus implying that he was a man of wealth and property. Stephanus (1 Cor. 1:16 and 16:15) was also in a position to devote himself to the support of Paul's work. We also know of Erastus (Rom. 16:23) who was the city treasurer.

We cannot always tell whether these people were Jews or Gentiles by birth but the existence of a number of Gentile names suggests that they were probably Roman citizens. 'They all', as Judge concludes, 'belong together as persons of substance, members of a cultivated social elite, and in particular as sympathisers with Jewish thought, since it was usually through the synagogue connection that they met St. Paul. They are the "devout and honourable" citizens of the Hellenistic states.'[16]

Many of the problems at Corinth can be understood in the light of the fact that people from different social classes still found it difficult to relate to each other even after their conversion to Christianity. They would be aware that, as far as God was concerned, such distinctions were no longer of any importance (1 Cor. 7:22; Col. 3:4) and yet in reality mutual acceptance still had to be learned through hard experience.

A review of the First Epistle demonstrates how these social distinctions displayed themselves at Corinth. The quarrelling and divisions of Chapter 1 may well have been an expression of cultural differences with the preaching of Apollos appealing to the more educated; the preaching of Cephas to the traditional Jews and the preaching of Paul, with its more direct style, appealing to the more common folk. Preachers today still find that their style and approach makes them more popular with certain types of people than with others. From 1:18 onwards Paul requests those with social and intellectual gifts not to place their confidence in these human qualifications but in the cross of Christ. Is it not likely that they had been guilty of looking down their noses at the others in Corinth who failed to enjoy their social advantages? Paul tells the superior members that if they must boast they can legitimately boast only as

Christians in Christ. Having made the point, he further develops it by dealing with the issue of wisdom (2:1–16) whose keenest proponents would have been the more cultured members of the Corinthian Church.

The issue of self-conceit continues to be the subject of the next two chapters. It could be that the basis for this feeling of superiority on the part of some was that they had received an esoteric revelation of God but it could equally be that they felt superior because, according to human standards, they were superior (4:18; see also 2 Cor. 5:16). Paul certainly displays a sensitivity to those of higher birth. For example, when he wishes to speak to them concerning his work as a servant of Christ (4:1, 2) he does not make the point in an undiplomatic way by talking of himself and Apollos as slaves (*doulos*) but as stewards and servants, which are more polished words. Throughout he speaks of himself and them as *diakonos*, *huperetes* and *oikonomos*. So he removes the prejudicial barriers the middle class members might have erected and creates an atmosphere in which his message can be readily heard and understood.

On another matter too it is probable that Paul was essentially speaking to the wealthier Christians. In 6:1f it becomes clear that some members of the church had taken other members to the law courts. Paul deprecates the practice and insists that any issues in dispute should be settled by the Christians internally, just as the Jews would do. Justice may in theory have been equally available to all but, in practice, just as in our own day, the more wealthy and articulate find it easier to make use of the means by which justice is administered. The issue over which the dispute had arisen was *biotikos*, i.e. every day affairs or matters which relate to the present life. Paul clearly uses the word to draw a contrast between the affairs of this world and the affairs of the next (v. 2). Even so it is also legitimate to see here a reference to 'material interests' and in this light it is highly improbable that the lower classes would even have been able to resort to litigation in the interests of their material possessions, whereas it is quite consistent with a middle class life style that members of that class would resort to law.

In the next section of the epistle the matter of status is again not too far from the surface. Ostensibly Paul is discussing the expediency of marriage and the proper conduct of a believer within marriage (1 Cor. 7:1–16). But he moves from this specific issue to the more general guidelines that a Christian should be happy to accept the position and status which is his lot in life without straining at the leash for a different situation. It is here that Paul refers directly to the issue of social status (v. 22) and shows that no status whether high or low is a barrier either to acceptance or usefulness in the church of God. Paul does not advocate the removal of these distinctions but their lack of importance and their reinterpretation in the light of what Christ had done.[17]

The next issue Paul raises is that of meat offered to idols. In this discussion he contrasts the 'strong' with the 'weak' (8:7–12, see also Romans 14). The strong are those who have knowledge (v. 4–7) and consequently realise that idols do not refer to anything which is real and so they eat meat which is offered to idols with a free conscience. The 'weak' are those who are unable to see idolatry in this light and whose consciences dictate that they refrain from any practice which might suggest that they were compromising their faith. Given the patterns of association which would lie behind this issue, it is a fair assumption on Theissen's part that the 'weak' ones would be the poorer members of the church and the 'strong' ones would be the richer and more educated members who were used to easy mixing and socialising.

It is when Paul comes to the issue of their behaviour at 'the Lord's supper' that the problem of social divisions are referred to most explicitly. At the very gathering at which the words spoken by Jesus on the night of his betrayal were repeated there was a marked contrast between two groups of people; one group were hungry but the other had so much as to be actually drunk (11:21). The actual circumstances of the meal are not entirely clear. Among the many suggestions as to how the meal proceeded there is that of Theissen[18] in which he supposes that the owner of the house would invite all Christians of whatever social class to share in a simple supper of bread and wine. The problem arose because in addition to that the hosts would invite their own social equals to a better meal which might have been enjoyed before the poorer people came from their day's work. It is not entirely clear how this is consistent with Paul's assertion that 'each one goes ahead with his own meal'.

Whatever the precise practice, it was, as often today, over eating and drinking habits that the divisions of the church came to light and so destroyed the very unity of which the common meal spoke. Paul proposes that unity should be made a central feature of the service and makes a practical suggestion that any other form of meal should be reserved for the privacy of home (11:33f).

It may be that the issues of charismatic gifts was not un-related to class divisions although here the evidence is by no means convincing. Sociologists have often tried to suggest that certain spiritual gifts such as speaking in tongues are parti-cularly suited to those who feel at least relatively deprived.[19] The socially or economically disadvantaged are said, there-fore, to find emotional release in the more expressive of the gifts of the Spirit mentioned in 1 Cor. 12. On this questionable foundation the theory is erected that at Corinth the lower classes were so enthusiastic in their use of spiritual gifts that they were not amenable to control by those who acted as their hosts. The hosts, i.e. the houseowners, would almost inevit-ably be men of some education with a fairly broad background and administrative abilities. They would be attracted, it is said, by the gifts of teaching, leadership and pastoring.

Paul obviously wishes to restrain the over-enthusiastic use of certain spiritual gifts and to establish a certain order of precedence in which the gifts of apostleship, prophecy and teaching come before miracles, healings and speaking in ton-gues (12:18–30). After the hymn concerning love, Paul returns to the question of tongues to emphasise again that this valu-able gift must not assume more importance in the Christian assembly than it really had. Clifford Hill has commented that the three gifts Paul places first in his list are gifts which require some exercise of intellectual abilities and that conse-quently the list is middle class in orientation.[20]

Given the presuppositions of this theory, it does explain the difficulties which Corinth was experiencing over spiritual gifts. It is, however, only an assumption, however logical, that the lower classes were attracted to the exercise of some gifts and the middle classes to the exercise of others, and unfor-tunately it is an assumption that recent research and experi-ence has not altogether confirmed.[21]

By now a general picture of the church at Corinth may have been obtained. In this socially heterogeneous church the leadership fell upon those who were middle class and elitist. They were the natural leaders, not only because of their social and educational skills, but because of their having the pro-perty in which to host the meetings of the church. Paul accepts their right to lead and supports them, both in that he baptised some of them (1:14f) and in what he says about spiritual gifts (given the reservations just expressed).

He is not happy, however, about certain attitudes they adopt or actions to which they are party. Much of 1 Corin-thians is a pointed address to them, encouraging them to overcome their deficiencies and forsake their worldly pretensions; however understandable these conceits may have been from a human standpoint. These activist leaders at Corinth needed to be wary lest they ran the church as they would an ordinary business and lest the working class people did not receive the standing in the church that God intended them to have. Paul was not arguing that the social distinctions should be completely abandoned by Christians any more than the biological differences between the sexes disappeared when people became Christians. But he was arguing that the church was an alternative society which operated on different principles from the normal society and enjoyed entirely new relationships. Within the church there must be acceptance and respect for people whatever their class background and the acknowledgement that God may use some prominently within the church who would not normally have risen to positions of leadership. In a word, the prominent members of the Church at Corinth needed to repent of their snobbery and treat the ordinary members with more seriousness.

A serious look at the data concerning the membership of the early church reveals it to have been a socially mixed movement. It certainly did not appeal simply to one class; be that the middle or the working class. Acts, Romans and 1 Corinthians all demonstrate the existence of middle class people. Many of them are mentioned by name and without their support Paul would have been unable to carry out his itinerant ministry. As well as these there were clearly also many from lower classes who, whether slave or free, enjoyed the privilege of belonging to the church. This social mix inevitably made for problems in a society which was renewed but still human and far from perfect. Learning to live in peace and harmony with those of differing social and cultural backgrounds is still a very difficult problem for the church. But it is an essential characteristic of the church that its members at least want to try to remove the social barriers which ordinary society loves to erect. And it remains a battle against worldliness in which there is never a ceasefire.

CHAPTER EIGHT

The Early Church's Relationship to the World

The subject of New Testament ethics is a discipline in itself and one strays into its territory therefore with some trepidation. Nonetheless a complete review of the sociological features of the early church must include some reference to the way in which the New Testament writers handled issues of personal morality, social relationships and political concern. It is wrong to think of the early church solely as a pliable community of people moulded by the pressures of their contemporary society. Their own religious belief led them to adopt ethical ideas and practices and consequently, even if they were not conscious of doing so, led them to influence the shape of the society of which they were a part.[1]

Before looking at specific issues a number of questions must be raised about the nature of New Testament ethics. We must ask how important ethical issues were to the New Testament writers; what kind of issues interested them; why their pronouncements have an *ad hoc* nature about them and what explanation can be given to the diversity of views expressed.

Judging by the amount of space devoted to ethical considerations the authors of the New Testament were very concerned about how Christians should live in the world. Once a new congregation had been founded they spent much time guiding its members as to how their new-found faith affected the whole range of their relationships and obligations. They immediately subjected the life-style of their converts to detailed scrutiny and placed high standards of morality before them.

For the most part this ethical teaching concerned personal rather than social issues. One looks in vain for a thorough political manifesto in the New Testament. The reason for this must in part be that the wider issues of government and social or economic policy were not the concern of the average member of the Roman Empire. Even if interest in these issues had been aroused the ordinary person stood no chance of influencing the political system. The applied teaching of the New Testament therefore deals with the world as the early Christians experienced it. It would have been pointless had it done otherwise. Just as the horizon for many people in pre-industrial England may well have been limited by the boundaries of their own village, so the limits of vision for many in the early church was confined to their own household community. It is then on the issues of personal morality and social relationships within the family and at work, issues closest to home, that the New Testament concentrates.

This also explains why there is no well-worked out system of ethics and why there is a certain *ad hoc* nature about the ethical teaching of the New Testament. A basic consensus is apparent concerning the topics which should be found on any church's ethical syllabus as we can see from the similarities to be found in Gal. 5:16–22; Eph. 5:3–20; Col. 3:5–17 and 1 Pet. 2:1f and also in Eph. 5:21–6:9; Col. 3:18–4:2 and 1 Pet. 2:18–3:7.[2] But there is also a great variety of topic and the syllabus is far from cut and dried. Paul spends much of his time in 1 Corinthians answering ethical questions which, whilst not unique to them, were uppermost in the minds of the Corinthian believers whilst not so crucial to others. Similarly James deals with issues on which others are silent and does so in his own vigorously penetrating style. The ethical teaching then was partly shaped by the needs and situations of particular local Christian communities.

In addition to the variety of topic there is also evident a diversity of perspective between and even within the writers about any particular issue. J. L. Houlden's book *Ethics and the New Testament* gives a precise statement of the diversity which can be found and also gives a summary account, from the standpoint of modern critical scholarship, of the reasons for it. Houlden argues that a particular author's approach to ethics is shaped by the interaction of two main doctrinal issues. Firstly there is the author's attitude to the second coming of Christ. If Christ's return is believed to be very near then little real attention is given to ethical teaching since the church will not be enmeshed in worldly concerns and social relationships for long. If however, the New Testament writer believes the coming of Christ to be delayed more serious and detailed attention is given as to how Christians should live in the world.

The second factor is the author's attitude to the world. The less valuable the world is to the author the less attention is paid to ethics. But if the church is seen to be merely a part of God's wonderful creation and if God is seen to remain comprehensively involved in all his creation, then ethical considerations become more prominent.[3]

Houlden sees the greatest inconsistency in the New Testament to lie not between the various writers but within one man, Paul. Paul builds his ethical teaching mostly on a doctrinal foundation but sometimes falls back on standard forms of conventional ethics. He sometimes argues from the belief that Christ's return is imminent and sometimes is happy to enforce day to day norms without reference to the second coming of Christ,[4] as his belief in the imminence of Christ's return apparently dies away.

The diversity must be accepted but not exaggerated. Houlden raises important issues concerning the shaping of New Testament ethics which go far beyond the scope of this book. Some would believe that he overstates the ethical diversity because he overstates the doctrinal inconsistency between and within authors. Paul's belief in the imminence of the second coming is a much debated point, for example, and some would credit Paul with greater consistency of view than Houlden does.[5] This in turn affects one's view of how coherent his ethical teaching was. It can be argued that an unchanging foundation for Paul's ethical teaching is that the Lord is 'at hand' and that this is not a question of the timing of his coming but of the way in which, however long his return might be delayed, the future has momentous implications for how we live in the present.

Whilst however one wishes to qualify some opinions about the diversity of teaching and attitude to the world the fact of diversity remains and reflects in part the situation in which the authors were writing. The issue is best further examined with reference to some specific issues as we shall see later in the chapter.

A GENERAL SOCIOLOGICAL ORIENTATION

Having set the general theological stage with regard to ethics we now add to its scenery some further sociological comments. Consideration was given earlier to the fact that sociologists view the early church as a sect.[6] Now we return to the framework which the sociology of sectarianism provides in order to examine the early church's approach to the world of which it was a part.

It is one of the primary characteristics of sects that they are jealous in guarding their purity. They wish to remain separate and pure from the stains of the world. No religious group can completely avoid contact with the world, although, let it be said, some make a good attempt at it. Whatever the degree of contact or isolation, the very existence of the world demands that sects adopt some attitudes towards it, promulgate some rules concerning their members' relationship to it and conceive strategies which will keep those members pure. Bryan Wilson has used the different orientations to the world which can be seen in today's sects as the criterion by which to distinguish the various types of sect that exist.

Wilson has distinguished seven different attitudes to the world. The *conversionist* sect believes the world to be evil and believes that individuals need to be rescued from it and that their conversion will mean a total transformation of the self. The *revolutionist* believes that the only way to deal with the world's evil is for the world to be totally destroyed. The destruction will come about by supernatural means. The *introversionist* sect finds the path of salvation within its own community in which a convert can be either insulated or isolated from the world. The *manipulationist* reinterprets the world and says that things are not what they seem and by providing a new perspective enables its adherents to cope with evil. The *thaumaturgical* sect relieves the evils of the present world by supernatural means such as the working of miracles. The *reformist* sect accepts the world but seeks to amend it and improve its social organisation. Finally, there is the *utopian* sect which teaches that the world can be remade and utopia ushered in by man's own human effort.[7]

When this analysis is applied to the New Testament it is seen that the early church did not conform to any one of these approaches exclusively. Even today it is probably wrong to assume that one response is to be found in pure form in any one sect to the total exclusion of the other responses. In New Testament days such strong compartmentalisations certainly do not fit.

Only one response is totally absent from the New Testament; that is the *utopian* response. Nowhere do the early Christians display any confidence in the idea that man, by his own means, can transform this world into a second paradise. The Kingdom of God is to be brought in by God. The strong emphasis on sin and its deep destructive effect on man, his nature and his world prevents the early Christians from placing any hope in man himself.

There is also little evidence of the reformist approach in the New Testament. We have already acknowledged that there is no well worked out programme of social or political improvement and that the improvement of the world at large is not a major concern. However, the reformist orientation is not altogether absent. As we shall see in relation to slavery, the early Christians quite consciously reformed the generally accepted institutions by altering their nature from within. Whilst they did not actively campaign for the abolition of such institutions and their replacement with new patterns of social organisation, they certainly did not leave them untouched and unimproved. There is also evidence that they did not view the world as wholly evil (1 Tim. 4:4, 5). Certain institutions, such as government, were in fact God-ordained structures and even if they did not always work in an ideal way, they were to be accepted and treated in a manner which would bring out the best in them (Rom. 13:1–7 and 1 Tim. 2:1, 2). And as has often been shown, the implication of the doctrines in which they firmly believed was that Christians, wherever possible, would be involved in the reformation of the world.

The other five responses are however all apparent. The conversionist and revolutionist responses are the most significant. There is, despite the belief that the world is not totally evil, an underlying belief that there is no lasting worth in this world. It is on its way to destruction and the ultimate answer is to be found in the new order of creation. The implication of this for the individual is that he must turn away from the life-style which has invited this destruction (Eph. 2:1–3, 1 Pet. 4:1–5) and be saved (Eph. 2:4–10). This conversion initiates the individual into a totally new life (2 Cor. 5:17) and guarantees that he is delivered from the corruption which will inevitably follow for the rest of mankind (Rom. 1 and 2; James 5:1–6; 1 Pet. 1:3–5 and Jude). It also places upon the convert entirely new ethical and moral obligations which are not accepted by the society at large (Rom. 12:11–15:7; Gal. 5:16–6:6; Eph. 4:17–6:9; Col. 3:1–4:6 etc.). This new status of conversion carried with it profound ethical implications. It was because they were converted people that they 'must no longer live as the Gentiles do' and because they are 'God's chosen ones' that they were to exchange their former lifestyles for new ones.

At the same time the whole of New Testament ethics is coloured by the belief that Christ is going to return to the world and that following his return the old world order will be totally destroyed and replaced by a new creation (Rev. 21). This revolutionist response is evident in Paul and Hebrews as well as more obviously in the apocalyptic writings of Peter, Jude and Revelation.

Paul explains to the Roman Christians, in the middle of his long ethical discourse (13:11–14), that it is precisely because the end times are near that one has to behave in a particular way. The Christian believers should already live as they will live in the new creation. Paul recognises that Christians will not be able to live up to the standards completely (12:18) and also that the expected change of environment will in itself bring about major changes in social relationships. Nonetheless the Christian community is to anticipate by its social behaviour the renewed creation that is yet to come.[8] The future return of Christ not only determines the Christian's general attitude (as in 1 Thess. 5:1–11) but also dictates certain particular issues. So in 1 Cor. 6:3–6 where Paul is condemning Christians for taking each other to court, he does so on eschatological grounds. They will one day judge angels and the world and consequently they should be able now to handle this matter internally. Their future role determines their present practice. This same approach is also to be seen in James (5:7, 8) and Hebrews (13:14–16).

The revolutionist attitude to the world is of course most easily seen in 2 Peter, Jude and Revelation. The connection between ethics and eschatology is evident in Peter's exhortation, 'Since all these things are thus to be dissolved, what sort of persons ought you to be in lives of holiness and godliness . . .' (2 Pet. 3:11). It must be admitted, however, that the primary focus of these teachings is not on ethics. The authors are too caught up with the thought of the overthrow of the present world to dwell too long on how people should behave within it.

Sanders in his work *Ethics in the New Testament* has argued that these writings are late attempts to resuscitate an already dying belief in imminent eschatology within the church. And he argues that the tone of these writings is fantastic in comparison with the comparative eschatological teaching of Jesus and Paul. But we have already seen how important the millennial hope was in the teaching of Jesus, even if its importance has been overestimated by some. The images of destruction are more extensive than they were in the teaching of Jesus and Paul and isolated from other aspects of Christian teaching, they stand out with a new and vivid starkness. But they are not inconsistent with the earlier teaching or teaching which comes from the middle period of the New Testament era.[9]

Sanders further criticises these writings by saying that they turn the Christian congregations into passive spectators of cosmic events and have no real reference to ethics. He goes so far as to say that 'this retreat from the ethical dimension . . . is the basic evil of the Apocalypse'.[10] Any ethical implication he does discover he regards, as purely formal and 'a last ditch sanction'. But two points need to be borne in mind which Sanders does not appear to consider. Firstly, there are many implications concerning the believer's relationship with the world which are inherent in these apocalyptic books. The emphasis is missed, however, not because no ethical implications exist but because they are not implications of a particular ethical kind. John stresses the need for purity and for the church to refuse to compromise. He speaks of the value and necessity of suffering. He gives them a reason to endure persecution. And he deals with the issue of competing centres of power in the world and argues that God alone is the ultimate source of authority. This surely is ethical teaching.

Secondly, it is unfair of Sanders to condemn Revelation for not being an ethical manual when clearly that was not its purpose or intention. True the usual ethical issues are left untouched but it would have been pointless to dwell on them when the very survival of the church was the issue at stake due to the vicious persecution initiated by Domitian. The purpose of the book was different from that of other books in the New Testament and must be judged by what it, not they, was trying to accomplish.

Gager has assessed the significance of the book more correctly in seeing that it weaves an alternating pattern of two sets of symbols which concern victory versus oppression.[11] The book is a therapy by which Christians persecuted in the real world can overcome their present circumstances by substituting for their everyday experience what they believe to be a greater reality; the millennial hope and the reign of Christ. It is this hope that enables them to keep believing when present realities would suggest that they would be wiser to give up their faith.

Unfortunately Gager refers to this hope as a myth—a word which bristles with problems. His presupposition is that the millennium predicted by Jesus had failed to occur and that this reassertion of millennial hope will shore up only temporarily the faith of an otherwise dispirited people. It was a technique to deal with the precarious nature of their belief when compared with the real facts. But, as mentioned earlier, it is not an unquestionable fact that the early Christians had been disappointed by the failure of Christ to set up utopia within their lifetime. And the early Christians regarded the return of Christ to reign, not as mythical truth, but as truth which one day would receive literal historical fulfilment even if they were unable to predict the day.

The conversionist and revolutionist responses to the world then are major themes in the writings of the early church. The three other responses which are also present may be mentioned more briefly.

The eschatological perspective of Paul already mentioned clearly has implications for an introversionist response to the world. The early Christians were to be the first fruits of the Kingdom of God on earth. Their corporate lives were to be a foretaste of the corporate life they would eventually experience in heaven. Belief could not be a privatised response to the good news of Jesus for God's intention had been to create a new society 'which stands out in bright relief against the sombre background of the old world'.[12] For the early Christians this did not mean, on the one hand, that salvation was to be found merely through membership of their particular community. On the other hand, the community was not irrelevant to their salvation. Nor did it mean that the early Christians cut themselves off from the wider world. Paul recognised that even to try to do so was fruitless (1 Cor. 5:10). They were very much members of the wider non-Christian society whilst at the same time they were ever-conscious of the need to keep pure even whilst living within it.

The manipulationist dimension is not as great in degree as it is in some modern sects such as the Christian Scientists. Yet to some degree the Christians did reinterpret their experiences in this world. Suffering is an obvious example. Christians came to treat it as a privilege (Phil. 1:29) and a joy (James 1:2) because to suffer was to identify with Christ (Rom. 8:17; Col. 1:24); to make progress in sanctification (Rom. 5:3–5) and to be able to look forward to future reward (Rom. 8:17; 2 Thess. 1:5–10).

Lastly there is some evidence of the thaumaturgical response as well. Christianity was certainly not in its early days a thaumaturgical sect which provided easy and immediate cures for all the evils of the present life. They did not regard the miracle of healing as the automatic and universal response every time someone was ill (e.g. Epaphroditus, Phil. 2:25). Yet miracles were worked as the Acts of the Apostles shows. These miracles were not limited to healings but included deliverance from shipwreck and miracles of judgment. The presence of miracles and healing in the list of the gifts of the

Spirit (1 Cor. 12:8–10) is also evidence that they were in wider operation. To that extent the early church responded to the world thaumaturgically.

The ethics of Christian discipleship then was not a rigid and inflexible set of dogmatic responses which could be automatically put into operation by any Christian anywhere as soon as he had had time to consult the rule book. They were much more a living application of various Christian doctrines and principles as the occasion demanded.[13] Sometimes the situation demanded an emphasis on the conversionist approach and sometimes the emphasis was on a revolutionist approach or on one of the other responses to the world. But always they were a clear application of the apostolic teaching and divinely revealed principles.

THREE SPECIFIC ISSUES

It would be possible to demonstrate the above by reference to many ethical issues which concerned New Testament Christians. We shall limit ourselves, however, to the attitude to the state, slavery and wealth.

(a) The State

A first glance at New Testament teaching regarding the state suggests that a wide variety of approach is to be found. In the Acts there is opposition between Church and State (Acts 4:19) but there is also an acknowledgement of how helpful the state can be to the church (e.g. Acts 25:13–27). Luke, in general, in his Gospel and the Acts tries to convince the authorities that there is no reason why they should not tolerate the church, with the result that he has been accused of 'establishment attitudes'. Paul subsequently stresses the need for Christians to be submissive to the authority of the state as a matter of principle (Rom. 13:1–7) and to support secular authority by prayer because it assumes a God-ordained role (1 Tim. 2:1–2). Peter also argues for Christian submission but the motivation for submission has changed (1 Pet. 2:13) to some degree. The motivation is not necessarily submission out of principle, but possibly submission because in that way the consequences of disobedience can be avoided (3:13). In the Revelation of John the situation is entirely different. The state is denounced as evil and in opposition to God and fit only to be overthrown and destroyed by God's judgment.

In the light of this it is right to ask if there is any coherence in the New Testament attitude to the state. Cullmann's examination of this question leads him to answer that throughout the New Testament 'one and the same fundamental attitude' towards the state can be detected, whether the speaker or author be Jesus, Paul, Peter or John.[14]

What is this attitude? Firstly, there is never 'an unconditional and uncritical subjection to any and every demand of the state'.[15] The state is always subject to the authority of God and is the servant of God (John 19:11; Rom. 13:1, 4) and it has therefore no ultimate and absolute authority which must not be challenged. It is never seen as infallible or omnicompetent. Further, it is the principle of the state, not individual rulers who may be unworthy holders of an office, that Paul has in mind. Secondly, the state does, however, perform a right and proper function in this world and is ordained by God for that purpose. Its function is basically a judicial one. When it is fulfilling this role it is right for Christians to give it what it demands (Mt. 22:21; Rom. 13:6–7). Given this role, the state has a certain dignity and is worthy of respect.

Paul does not directly face the question as to what one's attitude should be once the state steps beyond its powers and assumes the place of God himself and adopts totalitarian attitudes. His personal experience of Roman authority was that it had helped not hindered his ministry. And his positive attitudes are reflected in Romans 13 which was written before Nero's persecution began. Even when the state moved against him personally (2 Tim. 4:6), Paul sets this particular experience against the background of having largely received good at the hand of the authorities. So here he does not become condemnatory in his attitude to the state but rather accepts the rough with the smooth and trusts his life to God (2 Tim. 4:8 and 18). One must not press this argument too far or else one must conclude that all that Romans 13 contains is Paul's own opinion derived from his subjective experience, whereas in fact Paul is speaking of general principles and relating the institution of government back to divine basics.[16]

It is not at all inconsistent with these principles that Peter, writing in the different circumstances of growing threats to the Church, should still encourage obedience to the state but in a less wholehearted manner. Still the respect for authority is evident (1 Pet. 2:13–17) and submission to it is advocated. Nevertheless he has to begin to justify and explain how to handle the state's action when it apparently moves, not against evil but against good. (1 Pet. 3:13–17). In such circumstances there is a growing emphasis on the authority of Jesus Christ in contradistinction to the authority of the state.

This contrast reaches its climax as the state moves further and further beyond its God-given role and tries to assume deity itself. This is the situation behind the book of Revelation which was possibly written in the midst of the Domitian persecution. Here there are clear indications that the rulers of the state wish to place themselves in the very place of God (Rev. 13:1–4) and attempt to do so by imitating him. As a direct consequence of their action, they place themselves in direct opposition to God and John warns that such action cannot possibly succeed in anything but short-term and will not be tolerated by the ultimate authority in the universe. Emancipated human authority is satanic, not divine, and as such will receive the judgment of God. As Cullmann says,

> Now we understand why we hear a tone quite different here from that in Romans 13. In all other points the Johannine Apocalypse may be a book radically different from the Epistle to the Romans; but in the interpretation of the state there is no contradiction . . . Regarding the State's requirement of worship of Caesar's image Paul would not have spoken otherwise than the author of the Johannine Apocalypse.[17]

(b) Slavery

If the teaching about the Christian attitude to the state demonstrates a range of responses from a basically accepting attitude to a revolutionist, but not utopian, response, the attitude towards slavery is essentially one, that is, manipulationist.

Paul may well have arrived in Rome a year after the Proletarian riots of 61 AD. The riots followed the murder of the city prefect, Pedanius Secundus, who was also the owner of 400 slaves. The law stated that if slaves failed to prevent the murder of their master, they shared in the guilt of his murder and were therefore liable to capital punishment. Many senators argued that the law needed to be relaxed but some hard-liners, such as Gaius Cassius, continued to argue that, 'You will not restrain the scum except by terror.' The hard-liners won the day and the slaves were executed. As a Roman citizen Paul would not have been unaware of such happenings.

Yet people have searched in vain to find some teaching in Paul which condemns the institution of slavery and encourages Christians to work for its overthrow. Why is such explicit reformism absent? The answer must be twofold.

In the first place the institution of slavery was such an integral part of the social fabric of Paul's day that it would have been difficult for Paul or others to conceive of social organisation without it. Only the Essenes failed to accept slavery;[18] everyone else took it for granted. It was possible to accept slavery in this manner because by the time of Paul it was not a severe and cruel institution. Of course there were exceptions such as the incident recorded above, but the experience of most slaves was very different. In Carcopino's memorable phrase, 'With few exceptions slavery in Rome was neither eternal nor, while it lasted, intolerable . . .'[19]

More and more humanitarian legislation had been introduced in the first century AD; a trend which continued into the second century. Among the specific legislation was that of Claudius who ordered slaves abandoned by their masters to be manumitted; Nero who ordered complaints by slaves to be heard by the city prefects and Domitian who in AD 83 prohibited castration. Freedom became generally easier to obtain and even where it was not obtained, a slave could find himself with a master, like Pliny, who can only be described as having an indulgent attitude. From a slave's viewpoint then, the Roman social system could be seen as working in his best interests. There was no widespread discontent about slavery. So, to the early church the question of the abolition of slavery was probably insignificant.

The point has been well summarised by R. H. Barrow, 'Indeed,' he writes, 'slavery comes nearest to its justification in the early Roman Empire: for a man from a "backward" race might be brought within the pale of civilisation, educated, trained in a craft or profession and turned into a useful member of society.'[20]

Seen in this light, the persistent question as to why Paul did not openly challenge the institution of slavery seems to be very much a question that could be asked only by a twentieth century person fully conscious of the matter of human rights. But there is also a second aspect of the answer to consider. Paul did, in fact, challenge the institution of slavery but his challenge was directed to its inner meaning rather than its external existence. He gave to the converted slaves a totally new perspective on slavery and in that sense his approach to this particular ethical question was manipulationist. Unlike some manipulationists, Paul did accept the issue destined for reinterpretation as a physical fact. Some manipulationists pretend that the physical facts, e.g. suffering, do not really exist and are 'all in the mind'. Paul differs from them in this particular aspect.

What Paul offers to Christian slaves is a totally new appreciation of their value as persons. They are no longer 'things' but people who have standing and status before God (1 Cor. 7:20–24). In Christ the slave is a free man. God has demonstrated their worth by forfeiting the life of his Son through crucifixion. If only, Paul argues, they grasp this greater fact, slavery itself becomes inconsequential. A slave can remain happily a slave and still serve the Lord in spite of his social limitations. Such a view affects not only the slave's self-estimate but the actual pattern of relationships which exist between Christian masters and slaves. The letter Paul wrote to Philemon is a clear exposition of the new social relationships made possible through Christ.

Paul's instruction to the slaves to submit to their master must be interpreted in the light of this reinterpretation of their experience. They are to submit (Eph. 6:5–9; Col. 3:22–25 and also 1 Pet. 2:18–20) not because they are slaves of men but because they are more significantly servants of Jesus himself who will one day reward all men, whatever their social standing, with absolute impartiality. This call to submission must be seen also, not as a call to submit to a tyrannical and impersonal master, but one who is himself accountable to God (Eph. 6:9 and Col. 4:1) and one who, as leader of the household community, is well known and closely related to his slaves.

Paul's call for the early Christian slaves to accept and reinterpret their experience renders slavery itself 'almost, if not fully, meaningless' as commonly understood. Scholars have long debated whether this Christian reinterpretation ultimately led to the death of slavery in the Roman Empire. The balance of evidence is that it did.[21] Christian teaching, no doubt in diluted form as it became more common, entered the existing structures of society and gave them a new heart. The permeation of this new spirit meant that in the end the old existing structures could not continue unaltered.

(c) Wealth

Since the Jesus movement began in part as a millenarian movement which appealed to the economically insecure and demanded, at its beginning, from many, if not all of its disciples, a radical separation from property and riches, one looks with interest at the teaching of the early church about wealth. Again one finds that different responses are to be found, with one author stressing one aspect of the approach and a different author stressing another aspect. There is a basic underlying unity of approach however and the different stresses do not amount to contradictions.

Even in the Gospels different emphases can be found. These have recently been traced back to their sources by David Mealand who concludes that the different sources from which the Gospel writers drew their material reflects the economic situation in which that source of material was composed: the periods of economic difficulty resulting in greater structures against the wealthy. He identifies three periods of economic crisis for the early church, namely, the initial period when the church commenced; the famine of AD 48 and the worsening economic situation which led up to the Jewish revolt in AD 66.[22] These crises also, of course, formed the economic context in which Paul was working and writing and are reflected in his activities, especially in his concern for the economic plight of the church in Jerusalem.

Mealand concludes that Jesus' own attitude to riches was radical for he cared little for them and invited many of his disciples to leave them.[23] This radical demand should not, he says, be seen as a negative forsaking or severe sacrifice for the disciple. They themselves saw it as a matter of joy and approached it with a positive attitude.[24] But did this radicalism give way to compromise?

We have already seen that after the death of Jesus the early Christian community engaged for a brief while in a primitive form of communism. But this introversionist response was not to last for long and never became determinative in the attitude of the early church towards wealth.

Instead the early church continued to adopt a revolutionist and manipulationist attitude. Attacks on the rich and warnings about the way in which God will eventually judge them continue frequently in both early and late writings (James 5:1–6, 1 Tim. 6:17–19). They are warned throughout the New Testament period of the spiritual dangers of being rich (1 Tim. 6:6–10, James 2:1–7). God, it is taught, will bring the injustices of the present world to an end and a new just order will be introduced. The manipulationist element arises because the situations of the poor and rich are constantly reversed in New Testament teaching. Paul teaches that Jesus was rich but became poor so that the poor might become rich (2 Cor. 8:9). As with slavery he revolutionises standard values and stresses that a man who is poor in earthly terms may well be rich as far as God is concerned (1 Cor. 1; Phil. 3:20). The same theme is to be found in the letters to the seven churches (Rev. 2:9; 3:17, 18). Although it cannot be said that the epistles explicitly state the blessings of poverty in the same way in which the Gospel of Luke does their reinterpretation of poverty is entirely consistent with it.

Two other themes in the New Testament teaching on wealth relate to the conversionist and reformist responses a sect might make to the world. The conversionist response stresses that the way to overcome evil is to transform the individual. As far as wealth is concerned the New Testament looks for such a transformation among those who claim to be Christians. Unlike their contemporaries they are urged to be detached from possessions and to find their fulfilment and contentment in God alone (1 Cor. 6:12; Phil. 4:11f, 19). Such a conversion may have been particularly evident in one who had formerly been a thief by trade. Now as a Christian he was expected not only to be honest but to be generous (Eph. 4:28). But more than that, large-hearted generosity was expected of all, not just converted thieves (2 Cor. 8, 9).

It is in Paul's lengthy discussion in 2 Corinthians that the reformist strand comes out, although it stands on its own as far as the rest of the New Testament is concerned. Paul gives many reasons why the Corinthians should give generously for the needs of the church in Jerusalem and among them is the 'matter of equality' (2 Cor. 8:14). Paul can be thinking of equality in the Christian community only since economic reform on a wider scale was completely outside their sphere of competence. Nonetheless, Paul is not content simply to wait for the ushering in of the new age at the coming again of Christ. He urges the church to begin to live in the manner of that just society even in the present age.

Again then we must say that there is no systematic ethic available in the New Testament which can serve as a blueprint for social or political reform. Least of all does it give easy and direct answers to the pressing problem of the gap between rich and poor in our own industrial or post-industrial society.[25] Yet it must be said that the New Testament writers reveal attitudes and principles which when applied inevitably results in the righting of present injustices and the undermining of contemporary evils.

CONSERVATISM AND RADICALISM IN THE NEW TESTAMENT

The relationship between the early Christians and their social world has been approached in one further way which merits examination. But before embarking on that discussion it may be helpful to mention two matters which might clarify the implications of what has been said so far for Christian believers in the twentieth century.

Some have argued that the apparent lack of direct attention devoted to social and political issues in the New Testament absolves the present day believer from engaging in social amelioration or political debate. On the contrary, the implication of so much of the teaching which has been reviewed points to the need for Christians to be socially aware and active. This position is further supported if one takes the Old Testament into account as well as the New. The democratic context of our own society increases the obligation to participate in the affairs of the nation.

Secondly, the idea that New Testament ethics were essentially a response to problems which occurred then must not be overstated. It is true that the New Testament does not directly pronounce on many issues which are of primary ethical concern for us today. But it would be naive to expect the writings of the first century to comment on issues which had not even arisen in Paul's day; many of which have arisen because of man's subsequent technological advance. Nevertheless the New Testament remains relevant for our own day and is the basis on which a contemporary theology of ethics can be constructed. This is possible because, in spite of their varying responses to specific issues, the New Testament writers are not recording a merely personal opinion or superficial passing comment on matters. They are always concerned to relate the specific ethical issues back to more fundamental theological principles. So, to take a minor example, when Paul wishes to rebuke the church at Ephesus for its disunity, he does not do so by telling them that disunity is pragmatically unhelpful or personally uncomfortable but by pointing out that it is a denial of the unity which is to be found in their gospel and even in God himself (Eph. 4:1–6). Then he further shows them that there is a rightful diversity to be encouraged which is the result not of the accidents of personality but of the ministry of the Holy Spirit (Eph. 4:7–13).

Granting now that a Christian, motivated by theological concerns, ought to engage in social and political activities we are left with the question of how we should do so. One thinks now of the problem, forced upon us by our party political system, of the way in which one's views are channelled into a conservative or radical direction. For in spite of the widespread agreement that the New Testament does not contain any well worked out social or political programme, it is amazing how proponents of particular political parties attempt to legitimise their philosophies by reference to the New Testament. By a careful selection of the evidence and by turning a blind eye to the elements which do not fit, some have tried to make both Jesus and Paul a Conservative or a Socialist. A more balanced approach, however, is to be preferred because it is more congruent with what the New Testament itself says. The fact is that there are both conservative and radical elements to be found in its pages and that they are held in tension with each other.

Troeltsch[26] has examined this tension in some depth. Initially he seems to argue that the Jesus movement began as a very radical movement in respect of its social teaching but that with its growth and with the inevitable development of its relationship to the state it gradually compromised its radicalism until the point when it becomes conservative under Paul. The demands of their situation meant that Paul had to give the early Christians specific and concrete instruction in relation to the state and so Troeltsch concludes that 'Paul's ideas were quite distinct from the ideals of the gospel.'[27]

To stop reading Troeltsch's argument at this juncture, however, would lead to a total misunderstanding of his viewpoint. The argument develops through two other stages. In the next stage he stresses Paul's conservatism but also points out that whatever Paul's intentions may have been, his ethic actually exercised a revolutionary influence. The explanation for this lies in the fact that, despite all Paul's teaching regarding submission, he never gave unqualified loyalty to any existing social institution or unqualified obedience to its authority. Consequently, as we have seen in reference to slavery, his teaching had the effect of alienating souls from the ideals of the state.

The final stage of the argument is to examine whether the apparently revolutionary attitude of Jesus and the conservative attitude of Paul are in fact diametrically opposed to each other or whether they both derive from the same source and really belong to each other. Troeltsch is of the opinion that, 'Although both these tendencies may at times diverge very widely, they might perhaps still be united in an inward relationship, and form a united stream of development for the sake of the great ends to be realised.' 'The Pauline turn of thought,' he writes, 'in relation to social matters corresponds to the spirit and meaning of the Gospel.'[28]

The tone of Troeltsch's conclusion is somewhat cautious and even grudging. Due allowance has to be made for the process of institutionalisation, a phenomenon which will be examined in the next chapter. Due allowance also has to be made for the changed location of those who are being given ethical instruction. It would be foolish today to detail the same ethical application of the faith to a Suffolk farmer, a Surrey stockbroker and a Yorkshire miner. There will be common elements but also many different details. Similarly, different applications had to be made in detail to the rural Jewish followers of Jesus and to the city converts of Paul. However, when all such due allowances have been made, there is still a greater degree of unity in the ethical teaching of Jesus and Paul than even Troeltsch admits.

Both Jesus and Paul, who in any case derived his principles from Jesus, have a number of principles in common and these determine their respective ethical applications. Both believe in God as creator and sustainer of this world and both believe that he remains interested in his creation (Matt. 6:25–33; 1 Cor. 10:26; Col. 1:15–20; 1 Tim. 4:4). Both believe that the creation is subject to the judgment of God because of its fallen nature and therefore it is not to be accepted uncritically (Matt. 11:20–24; John 5:22-30, 9:39; 16:8–11; Acts 17:26–31; 1 Cor. 9:1–27). Both believe that ultimately this world is doomed to destruction and therefore man is not to find ultimate significance in the things of this world (Luke 12:15 and 23; John 4:34, 6:27; 1 Cor. 15:51–57; Col. 3:1–4; 1 Tim. 6:6–12). And both are convinced that it is possible for man to know God in this world with the result that he begins to live in a fresh manner as a member, even if a far from perfect one, of the community of love (Matt. 18:15–20; Mark 10:35–45; John 3:1–14; Eph. 4:17–5:1; 1 Thess. 4:1–12). These essential principles ensure that however much some have detected divergences between them, there is a basic unity which overrides all else.

Some of the statements of the Lausanne Covenant seem to summarise this unified position aptly:

Culture must always be tested and judged by Scripture. Because man is God's creature some of his culture is rich in beauty and goodness. Because he is fallen, all of it is tainted with sin and some of it is demonic. The Gospel does not presuppose the superiority of any culture to another, but evaluates all cultures according to its own criteria of truth and righteousness, and insists on moral absolutes in every culture . . .

We affirm that God is both the Creator and the Judge of all men. We therefore should share his concern for justice and reconciliation throughout human society and for the liberation of men from every kind of oppression. Because mankind is made in the image of God, every person, regardless of race, religion, colour, culture, class, sex or age, has an intrinsic dignity because of which he should be respected and served, not exploited . . . The message of salvation implies a message of judgment upon every form of alienation, oppression and discrimination, and we should not be afraid to denounce evil and injustice wherever they exist. When people receive Christ they are born again into his kingdom and must seek not only to exhibit but also to spread its righteousness in the midst of an unrighteous world. The salvation we claim should be transforming us in the totality of our personal and social responsibilities. Faith without works is dead.[29]

These clauses have distilled the essence of the unified New Testament position regarding social ethics and they preserve the balance that is to be found in the New Testament between a conservative and a radical approach. Either of these emphases cast adrift from each other is unfaithful to the early Christian position. Sadly there is a great need for contemporary Christians to rediscover this balance and to escape from current polarisations which are perhaps encouraged by our basically two-party political system. If only Christians could acknowledge their need of each other's insights perhaps, instead of engaging in internal fighting, they might once again change the inner spirit of the nation as their good old forefathers did.

CHAPTER NINE

The Process of Institutionalisation

The growth and change of an individual person is taken for granted. In today's world photographs and home-made movies trace a person's development from babyhood through childhood to the prime of youth. With less pride we can trace by the same means the progressive thinning of the hair, the increasing weight and the ever more noticeable stoop which we associate with the onset of middle age and the years beyond. We are less familiar with the process of ageing which takes place in organisations but it is a well observed and well documented phenomenon among sociologists; although this familiarity should not lead one into thinking that there is perfect agreement as to how the process can be analysed.

THE THEORETICAL FRAMEWORK

One analysis has been put forward by David Moberg on the basis of a thorough acquaintance with organisational theory and close observation of churches in America. His framework is a useful illustration of the various 'ages' of a church without claiming for itself that it is the only possible or correct framework. Moberg[1] identifies five stages.

First there is the stage of *incipient organisation*. This refers to the church's earliest days, its period of emergence where its structures are relatively formless and its life centres on strong, new leadership and when it may be generating a good deal of collective excitement. Secondly, it moves into a period of *formal organisation* during which phase the leadership attempts to impose a greater sense of cohesion on the movement. The leader does this by encouraging the commitment of people to the movement, probably through a system of membership which serves to mark his people off from others. Other forms of distinctiveness, e.g. ethical codes or religious practices, also increase in importance at this time. The third phase is seen as the period of *maximum efficiency*. Moberg associates this phase with increasing responsiveness in terms of recruitment, less emotionalism and more stability and the leadership being in the hands of statesmen. It is the period in which programmes and committees are well and responsively structured. This is followed by the *institutional phase*. Here bureaucracy develops to the point at which it exists merely to perpetuate its own interests. Leadership too is self-perpetuating. Little spontaneity is to be found anywhere in the worship of the church and belief is in a creed merely as a relic of past ages. The church no longer sees itself as very distinctive from those outside of it and toleration reigns. Uncorrected this stage eventually gives rise to the fifth and final stage of *disintegration* or decline.

Several aspects of Moberg's analysis provoke questions and yet the overall framework is recognisable. Eddie Gibbs has expressed the same process in more popular form in speaking of the way in which religious groups develop from *men* to *movements*, turn into *machines* and eventually become *monuments*.[2]

This pattern of change is called the process of institutionalisation. It is a general process and is not necessarily limited exclusively to Moberg's fourth phase. It is the process by which the activities, values, experiences and relationships of the group become formalised and stabilised so that relatively predictable behaviour and more rigid organisational structures emerge.[3] It is the name for the way in which free, spontaneous and living movements become structured and inflexible. It is naive to think that any movements can function without structures. Total freedom from structures is not even possible and even less desirable. Institutionalisation refers to structures, however, when they have ceased to function in the best interests of the movement they are supposedly serving.

The impact of this process is sometimes so vast as to cause the nature of the movement to undergo a radical change of form. Many a group which has started out as a vigorous conversionist sect has, as the second generation have taken over and as it has experienced growth in size and organisational complexity, become a much less aggressive denomination.[4] It is equally possible for the process of institutionalisation to operate within any one type of organisation so that a sect may become institutionalised without ceasing to be a sect and a denomination may be more or less institutionalised in form.

All social movements and organisations are prone to institutionalisation but perhaps religious movements are particularly vulnerable simply because they are religious. Religious movements often arise as a result of the extraordinary experiences of a charismatic figure. The experiences of these individuals may vary but in one way or another they believe themselves to be in touch with God or the ultimate in a way which is not experienced by the ordinary man in his run-of-the-mill religious activity. They may sense, as a result, that they are especially chosen or commissioned by God. On the basis of this call they begin to form a group of disciples who are prepared to commit themselves to this leadership. But the very act of having a following involves a number of implications which may, in fact, bring about institutionalisation.

To begin with the leader will wish to communicate his unique experience of the sacred and for him to express his experience in words may well change or reduce the experience since words may not adequately express its reality. It may well be, too, that in order to maintain his leadership and confirm his spiritual standing the charismatic figure will be under pressure from his followers to repeat what was the original and spontaneous religious experience. One miracle or one vision may be insufficient to continue the legitimacy of his authority, with the result that the repetition of the experiences may be more humanly induced or engineered than was the original. Again, the leader will wish his followers, at least his close followers, to experience the sacred for themselves, with the result that some who have not genuinely experienced it will act as if they have. The particular experience enjoyed by the leader will perhaps become the distinctive feature of this group, with the consequence that men will routinely claim it in order to merit membership in the group. There is also the point that all charismatically led groups face a crisis on the death or failing powers of the charismatic founder and have to opt for new forms of leadership.

The effect of this process is that as the unusual has been shared with others, the unpredictable and spontaneous elements have been tamed and routine elements have increased. Even charisma, which may still be there, has been restrained and men expect it to work in a certain way. It has become routinised. It is the peril of making a real experience of the sacred a common and ongoing experience for a group. The explanation lies in the fact that both groups and everyday life cannot function for long on the unpredictable. They need a certain amount of stability.

These seeds of organisational decay begin to flower as the movement passes beyond its original phase and as a second generation takes over the leadership. The important elements of this part of the process of institutionalisation have been penetratingly analysed by Thomas O'Dea who has identified five dilemmas which every religious institution faces.[5]

The first dilemma is that of *mixed motivation* which O'Dea sees as the achilles heel of social institutions. The movement begins with the charismatic leader displaying a rigid single-mindedness. His mission is clear and he does not deviate from it. But subsequent leaders begin to work for the movement for reasons other than just fulfilling its primary goal. Structures, roles and offices emerge to lend the movement stability. This opens the door to men to seek for leadership positions for reasons of self-interest. New motivating forces such as the desire for prestige or power begin to adulterate the leadership.

O'Dea has identified three aspects of the more advanced stage of this problem of mixed motivation. Firstly there emerges a careerism which is concerned only formally about the goals of the movement. Secondly, there is a growth of bureaucracy which is more concerned with maintenance and protecting vested interests than achieving the movement's original goals. Thirdly, the leadership becomes timid and lethargic rather than vital and progressive. Perhaps it would be helpful if the diversification of goals, which is so clearly implicit in this, was itself spelled out as a separate phenomenon.

The second dilemma O'Dea refers to as the *Symbolic Dilemma: Objectification versus alienation*. It has to do with worship and ritual. Originally worship is man's response to the inbreaking of the transcendent, but, for that to be repeated and shared, the sacred has to be expressed symbolically. The sacred therefore gets enshrined in ordinary human words, actions and objects and its repetition makes it prosaic. Its survival demands that it be stabilised in these established forms and procedures. But what happens is that the worshipper is in danger of responding to the ritual, the external instead of the sacred itself. In a subsequent stage the response of the worshipper becomes even less important and he may feel little impact from the ritual. The preservation of the ritual, its language and customs becomes the important issue and true worship, in the sense of a response to the sacred, no longer takes place.

Objectifying the sacred in symbolic form leads to the alienation of the worshipper from the sacred. O'Dea warns that the dilemma is inescapable for 'to symbolise the transcendent is to take the inevitable risk of losing the contact with it. To embody the sacred in a vehicle is to run the risk of its secularisation'.[6]

The third dilemma is that of *Administrative Order: Elaboration versus Effectiveness*. As charismatic leadership is routinized so bureaucratic structure increases with a number of consequences. The office and the incumbent of the office become more and more distinct and the personal worth of leaders less significant. Structures are erected to respond to a particular set of problems but are never dismantled. This means that more and more structures are developed and the movement's complexity increases. Original structures which were genuine answers to original problems may subsequently become a powerful hindrance to dealing with later problems. They may even be the cause of later problems. Communication becomes increasingly important but also increasingly difficult to maintain effectively. Roles, spheres of competence and authority begin to overlap between one department and another creating tensions and dis-ease. And these bureaucratic features are aggravated further by the mixed motives of the people involved to which reference has already been made.

Fourthly we have *The Dilemma of Delimitation: Concrete definition versus substitution of the Letter for the Spirit*. The second dimension spoke of the standardisation of worship. This dimension refers to standardisation on a broader scale. The original insights of the charismatic leaders become more and more stereotyped in their expression so that their followers can be certain about what is acceptable orthodoxy and what is not. Doctrine gets defined with increasing rigidity or even certain words or formulae are erected as the tests of soundness. Perhaps an even clearer illustration of the process relates to the matter of ethics. Many a movement has begun with a few simple basic principles and a stress on the spirit of those principles, only to find that they become defined more and more concretely as the time passes. No laws becomes new laws. And a new legalism emerges to replace the old legalisms which the movement was founded to destroy. Again O'Dea believes that such a process is unavoidable. But he also reminds his readers that the written code kills whilst the spirit gives life.

The last dilemma is that of *Power: Conversion versus Coercion*. The movement from conversion to coercion has a number of definable steps. Originally people join a movement because they are converted to it and the conversion is in no way adulterated. But the first step away from a movement relying on conversion as its means of recruitment comes when the children of converts also wish to join the movement. They are not so much converted to it as socialised or educated into it. If the movement grows and becomes popular the demands of membership may be lessened further. A fourth step occurs when the movement has become so widely accepted that it becomes allied to the wider culture. A fifth step takes place when church and culture are so identified that the church becomes the legitimator and preserver of the culture. The preservation of the church and the maintenance of public order are then one and the same thing. In this final phase conversion has been substituted by coercion and unbelievers are social and political as well as religious deviants.

The above picture is obviously painted in bold colours and the reality contains many shades in between. But the direction of the trend is discernible in movements throughout history. Again and again the choice has been between purity and power; purpose and popularity.

Putting O'Dea's thesis in simple terms we might say that movements are institutionalising when they are experiencing a fragmentation of goals; a mixing of the leader's motives; a ritualisation of worship; an undisciplined mushrooming of bureaucracy; a petrifying of definitions and a pursuit of power or popularity.

THE NEW TESTAMENT AND INSTITUTIONALISATION

Throughout his work O'Dea assumes a determinism which makes it impossible for a religious movement to escape these dilemmas and even less to face them and win through as a youthful and spontaneous movement. His pessimism may well be justified; history would largely suggest it is. Before, however, we examine how the threat of institutionalisation can be averted, we need to ask a prior question. Is there evidence of the process of institutionalisation in the New Testament? If so, was it recognised or ignored?

Plenty of scholars have detected the process within the early church. Troeltsch speaks for many in claiming that, 'During the time of Jesus' life on earth there was no sign of an organised community. A visible community was only formed after his death.' And that,

. . . as soon as a message of this kind creates a permanent community a social order will inevitably arise out of this programme and that a sociological structure which was at first conceived solely in religious terms will be transformed into a social organisation within life as a whole.[7]

It is worth making one observation on Troeltsch's view in passing. It is inadequate to adopt the position that a movement may begin for purely religious reasons but then be maintained by sociological forces. A sociologist will, if he is true to his discipline, seek to explain both the origin and continuance of the movement in sociological terms.

Be that as it may, in our examination of the process of institutionalisation in the early church we need to be aware that as far as the New Testament is concerned, we have evidence of development only for a fairly short period of time. The New Testament is written by and chiefly concerns the first generation of Christians. The second generation, with all their attendant institutional implications, have not yet taken over when its pages close although they are clearly in the wings and ready to enter the stage. One cannot therefore expect to find a great degree of institutionalisation. If we were to move beyond the scope of this present work into the subsequent period of church history, from the second to the fourth centuries, more obvious institutionalisation would be apparent. Even so, we have seen how early the process begins to work and within the New Testament period the original founder of the movement had already passed on its leadership to his disciples. We may therefore reasonably expect to find some evidence of the effects of institutionalisation however embryonic; it cannot be altogether absent.

In fact many New Testament scholars believe the process to be so advanced according to certain of the epistles that they have doubted whether these epistles could actually have been written by the apostle Paul in the first century as they claim to be. The letter to Ephesus and the Pastoral Epistles have come under suspicion in this respect. The theological arguments for and against their authenticity as works of Paul are complex but there seems to be no ultimately convincing reason to reject their authenticity and much seems to commend them as having early dates.[8] We shall assume their genuineness in the argument that follows and so examine them to see what evidence they offer of institutionalisation in the earliest period of the church.

First, there is the issue of leadership. Dunn says Ephesians

2:20 'is easily read as an expression of second generation veneration of first generation leaders'.[9] But alternative interpretations are possible and it is more probable that Paul is claiming no more here than that the church is founded on apostolic teaching—a claim made right from the start of the Christian church and even stated by Jesus himself (e.g. Matt. 16:18; Acts 2:42, 5:32; Gal. 1:6–2:21 etc.).

The fullest discussion of the question of leadership occurs in 1 and 2 Timothy and Titus and it is commonly claimed that these epistles show a picture of the ministry in a more advanced state of organisation and prominence than is previously apparent. This claim needs to be treated with caution and some of the exaggerated aspects of the argument must be rejected. It is not true, for instance, as some have claimed, that Paul was indifferent to the question of Church authority until he wrote these letters. Acts 14:25 demonstrates his earlier concern. Nor is it possible to substantiate the view that Timothy and Titus are being presented as monarchical bishops in the later mould of Ignatius.[10] They could quite well achieve all the tasks assigned to them merely as personal and informal apostolic delegates.

Yet there is some evidence of institutionalisation. Some argue that Paul here is no longer emphasising the charismatic leadership and lifestyle of an earlier day but is coming to terms with the more measured and regulated leadership of office-bearers. The informal dynamic is being replaced by a more formal structure. This position is based on 1 Tim. 3:1f where Paul outlines the 'office' of bishops (or elders) and deacons. The original Greek does not in fact refer to the 'office' at all. It simply says, 'if anyone desires to be an overseer'. The structural aspects of the task, which one would expect to see if institutionalisation was advanced, are still absent from Paul's thinking at this point.

The evidence of institutionalisation lies not so much in the emergence of a growing structure but firstly in the lessened emphasis on charisma (reference to the Holy Spirit is almost absent from these epistles) and secondly in the fact that the basic personal qualifications required of leaders need to be spelled out at all. In the earlier days leaders would have emerged with self-evident qualifications for the task. Now choices have to be made and some men who are presenting themselves or are being put forward by others for leadership do not measure up to the required standard. There is no explicit reference to men seeking a position for reasons of personal prestige (although this is the case with Diotrephes in 3 John 9) but it is a fair implication from what Paul writes that this was so. It may be legitimate too to see 1 Tim. 3:6 as evidence of Paul's desire to control the entry into the ministry which would be a further sign of institutionalisation. However, Paul never did thrust young men into leadership positions as can be seen from his relationship to Mark and Timothy himself and it may be that he is simply taking wise and practical steps to prevent dangerous developments. But the very need for caution and to protect the future of the church through safeguarding its leadership is some evidence of institutionalisation. The place of honour awarded to the leaders in 1 Tim. 5:17–19 also indicates some degree of institutionalisation.

The only evidence that there was any widening of goals of the early church comes not through a positive admission that diversification was taking place, but through Paul's insistence that Timothy keeps his aims clear (1 Tim. 1:18, 19; 4:7, 13-16; 6:11–12; 2 Tim. 2:1–7; 4:1–5). This insistence on Paul's part would have been unnecessary unless Timothy's single-mindedness was under threat.

As to the ritualisation of worship, again the New Testament is far from forthcoming. We know that by the time of Justin Martyr's *First Apology* in AD 150, Christian worship was fairly stylised. But spontaneity, within certain guidelines, seems to be the key with the New Testament itself and there does not appear to be any attempt to enforce one particular pattern or liturgy on the early Christians. Dunn stresses the element of diversity within the New Testament, saying that the unifying feature lay not in the form of worship but in its being centred on the exalted Jesus. He does, however, seem to overstate the diversity for he argues that in 1 Corinthians worship is entirely congregational and led by the Spirit and that Paul does not envisage any established leadership there, whereas he stresses that in the Pastorals worship is not a spontaneous congregational activity but a closely regulated and man-led activity.[11] This sharp contrast, however, ignores the stipulations Paul lays down in 1 Cor. 14:26–33 for orderly worship. Further, the evidence Dunn produces from the Pastorals (1 Tim. 2:12; 3:2; 4:13 and Titus 1:9) does not always seem to bear directly on the issue. He does acknowledge that in 1 Tim. 2:8 prayer is obviously still a congregational activity. Perhaps if Paul had been writing directly about worship in the Pastorals, the sprit of his writing would not have been so different from 1 Corinthians as Dunn believes. With the possible exception of the Lord's Supper, it does not appear that any repetitive ritual or inflexibly structured order of worship had emerged by the end of the New Testament era.

There is even less evidence of a growing bureaucratic structure in the New Testament. Of course absence of evidence does not mean evidence of absence and it may be that since it was not the primary concern of the New Testament to be a text book on church discipline, it simply does not refer to a bureaucracy which existed. Right from the beginning the apostles in Jerusalem did have mechanisms for responding to problems that were forced upon them. For example, in Acts 11:19–24 Barnabas was sent to scrutinise the new converts in Antioch and in Acts 15 a full church council is held to establish the right attitude towards Jewish regulations. But it is highly improbable that these reactions to particular problems ever became formal and lasting procedures or structures in the early church. Perhaps the attitude to widows (1 Tim. 5:9–16) and elders under suspicion (1 Tim. 5:17–21) is some evidence of an incipient bureaucracy.

On the question of doctrine there does seem to be a *prima facie* case for accepting the process of institutionalisation. Paul's use of the word 'faith' in the Pastoral Epistles is said to be uncharacteristic of him. Faith is no longer primarily an active trust in Christ but 'the faith' in the sense of a set of defined doctrines which are to be believed and preached (1 Tim. 1:19; 3:9; 4:1, 6; 5:8; 6:10, 12, 21 and 2 Tim. 3:8). Guthrie has pointed out that this usage of faith has earlier parallels (e.g. Phil. 1:27; Col. 2:7; Eph. 4:5 etc.) and the feature is not in fact altogether new. Further 'the faith' accounts for only nine out of the thirty-three uses of 'faith' in the Pastorals and Paul's other more typical uses of the word are not absent.[12]

Is it then true that earliest Christianity began as a widely diverse movement with respect to doctrine on which a gradual uniformity was gradually imposed? Dunn has recently argued as much and proposed the view that the only real unifying element was Jesus himself.[13] But granting that the New Testament is marked by diversity on many issues and granting still further that the limits of legitimate Christian belief were having to be defined within the New Testament period as new boundaries or issues are met for the first time, Dunn's position may still be questioned. From the earliest days there was evidently a doctrinal orthodoxy, a well developed central core of beliefs which defined whether one was a Christian or not. There was not a radically diverse, undisciplined or loose set of beliefs which were gradually squeezed into a mould of doctrinal uniformity in some form of linear development as the theory of institutionalisation suggests. The diversity was never that radical and the uniformity never that crippling in the time of the New Testament.

What of the evidence with regard to ethics? Can there be detected in the New Testament a move from 'no rules to new rules'? Paul, in his earlier writings such as Corinthians and even Romans, emphasises the importance of the spirit as opposed to the letter (2 Cor. 3) and argues for a mutual love and respect when Christians differ over certain ethical practices (Rom. 14 and 1 Cor. 8). At times he is prepared in these early writings to admit openly that no 'correct' rule has been revealed on certain matters (e.g. 1 Cor. 7:6, 25 and 40). Throughout the epistles there is a common core of ethical teaching which defines personal qualities which every believer was encouraged to demonstrate and social norms which should mark their relationships with each other and the non-believing world. But nowhere is this presented as a new legislative system. Legalism is always avoided. This is as much true of the Pastoral Epistles as other epistles. In fact at one juncture Paul explicitly appears to be condemning the legalistic attitude of some who, in his view, wrongly claim to be speaking as Christians (1 Tim. 4:1–5).

The last dilemma of institutionalisation, as outlined by O'Dea, was that of conversion versus coercion. Within the short period of the New Testament one could not expect that too much progress could have been made down this particular road. By the time of Constantine it was to be a different matter. But the New Testament itself ends with the church being coerced by the state, not itself coercing anyone into its fold. Two matters are discernible, however, that might indicate a move away from the purest position which demanded that membership could occur only on the basis of a radical conversion taking place. First, Titus 2:11, 12 seems to suggest that the Christian life is now a matter of socialisation; or that grace is now a matter of education. The rest of the epistle clearly shows that Paul has not in any way deviated from his usual doctrine of salvation by grace through faith and Titus 3:3–8 is as classic a Pauline summary of the gospel as one could find anywhere else in the New Testament. The training mentioned in Titus 2:12, it should be noted, does not lead to but leads from the grace of God.

Secondly the changing attitude to wealth may be said to indicate a blunting of the sharp division between the church and the world. Jesus, it is often said, demanded a life of poverty (e.g. Mark 10:17–31) and even James denounces the wealthy

(James 5:1–3), whereas Paul, by comparison, lays only minor obligations on those who are wealthy (1 Cor. 16:1f; 1 Tim. 6:9, 10, 17–19). The Pastorals, it has been said, 'evince what has been called a bourgeois attitude to Christianity, heavily weighted in favour of practical morality and conventional ethics.'[14] Does this suggest a growing compromise with the world in an attempt to make the membership of the church a less demanding and more tempting proposition? One can hardly answer that question positively if one reads the Pastoral Epistles with any degree of care. Paul's ethic with regard to property was from the beginning unchanging. He believed it to be potentially evil (1 Tim. 6:9–10) but not inherently so and equally he believed it to be potentially useful (1 Tim. 6:19; 2 Cor. 8 and 9). Regardless of this issue, in all other respects the Pastoral Epistles display Paul's deep consciousness of the battle situation the early Christians were in *vis-a-vis* the world. No spirit of compromise is apparent; rather everywhere continuing vigilance and warfare is urged (1 Tim. 1:18; 4:16; 6:12; 2 Tim. 2:3–4; 3:10–15; 4:1–5).

This review of the aspects of life in the early church which might demonstrate the degree to which institutionalisation has taken place has been somewhat guarded. That is because caution is in order. Most evidence for institutionalisation is implied rather than explicitly stated. Some degree of institutionalisation is apparent but not nearly as much as has often been suggested. It was inevitably at work but in a much less pronounced and more subtle way than has been represented in the past. Dunn, in particular, over-emphasises the degree of diversity and often imposes on Scripture a linear framework of institutionalisation rather than allowing Scripture to speak for itself. The brakes were not let off the process until after the end of the New Testament period where the growth of offices and bureaucracy, the stereotyping of worship, the legalisation of ethics and the intellectualising of Christianity became standard. it was in reaction to these petrifying trends that Montanism emerged. Nevertheless, Paul particularly was aware that institutionalisation was a threat and made strenuous efforts to encourage the future leaders of the church to escape it.

IS THERE AN ESCAPE?

It is foolish to think that any human structures can escape from the creeping paralysis of institutionalisation. Man's structures suffer from the effects of the fall as much as an individual or the world itself does. The history of the church is a history of repeatedly alternating patterns of institutionalisation and revitalisation. Sometimes the renewal has taken place within existing structures. More often the revitalising movement has been misunderstood by those who inhabit the existing structures and so it has been ejected from those institutions causing yet another institution to be born. Our world today is consequently littered with dead structures that no one has had the courage to bury.

Paul seems aware of this danger within the early church. In writing to Timothy he seems anxious to give him advice which will help to overcome the problem of institutionalisation. It consists chiefly of three principles. First he is to guard the original aim, teaching and life of the church (1 Tim. 1:19; 4:16; 6:20 and 2 Tim. 1:14). He is not to preserve its structures in a fossilised form but to hold fast to its principles, however flexibly he may apply them. He is to hold fast also to its message without deviating, however varied the expression of it may be. It is a frequent mistake by man to hold firm to the wrong things. In holding firm we must hold firm to principles and revealed truths, not to forms, traditions and structures which are vehicles that conveniently or aptly express those principles in any one age. Constantly the church needs to go back to the self-critical and painful task of asking itself what are its goals and aims and it needs to bring its structures and programmes into line with those aims.

Secondly, Paul urges Timothy to recognise his battle-torn circumstances and not to relax his vigilance (1 Tim. 1:18; 4:16; 6:12 etc.). The moment he ceases to believe that he is at war he will get caught up with all sorts of secondary issues and fail to satisfy his commander (2 Tim. 2:4). Part of the trouble with many churches today is that they no longer see themselves as in a battle situation. They demonstrate no alertness to what is happening to them and, accepting everything that comes their way, do not have any desire to make an impact on the world around them.

Thirdly, Paul reminds Timothy of the fact that the original spiritual resources are still available to him (1 Tim. 4:14 and 2 Tim. 1:6–7). He needs constantly to renew his own spiritual energies in order to maintain the stamina needed for the battle.

Institutionalisation can then be defeated only by regularly going back to basics and reviewing. We need to ask regularly what are our aims and how are we achieving them. We need to ask regularly if the best people are leading and if people are suited to the tasks we wish them to achieve. We need to be alert constantly to the peril of mixed motives, the threat of unwieldy bureaucracy, the lessening of standards and the fossilisation of principles. We might add too that the church needs to be always alert to new men through whom God may wish to lead it in the way of renewal. Above all, the church needs humbly and often to return to the source of all life and vitality, God himself.

CHAPTER TEN

Early Church Experience

To end a sociology of the early church where the New Testament itself ends is somewhat unusual. Most sociologists have looked at the early church on a longer time scale. One can understand the reasons for their fascination. The nature of the movement inevitably changed with the demise of the apostles and so sociologists have been interested to trace the process of institutionalisation on into the next generation and beyond. They have examined its growing popularity and hotly debated whether its success was an advantage or disadvantage, as judged by the terms of the original movement. They have also traced the social demarcations which led to the drawing up of the battle lines between orthodoxy and heresy.[1]

The continuing story of the church provides then much of interest for the sociologist, especially as with its development new sociological factors and forces have to be taken into account. But with the close of the canon of the New Testament a significant chapter in the early church's history has come to an end and so provides one with a suitable place to take stock.

We need to return now at the end of our journey to the question of the relationship between sociology and Christian belief. Hopefully the journey has not only been interesting but informative, resulting in a greater understanding of parts of the New Testament. Hopefully, too, it has been possible to learn some relevant lessons for today's church as the journey was in progress. This certainly is not the primary intention of the sociology of religion[2] but nonetheless the implications, especially for the growth of the church,[3] are there. The fundamental issue at stake, however, remains the apparent threat to religious belief mounted by sociological explanation.

To paraphrase Eileen Stevenson[4], the Christian looks back

on what happened through Jesus Christ and in the early church as unique and as the revelation of God. On the other hand, the sociologist appears to undermine this belief and treats what happened as merely human experience, which Christians have in common with many other men.

This threat to uniqueness is rendered even more serious if one accepts the insights of the sociology of knowledge which Robin Scroggs[5] has acclaimed as 'the single most important approach within the field of sociology' as far as the sociology of the New Testament is concerned.

The popularity of this approach owes much to the writings of Peter Berger and a brief exposition of his views is necessary at this point.[6] When a human being is born he encounters society as a real phenomenon. It is objective, given and seems to be factually there. It compels his recognition and coerces him to behave in certain ways. This social world is so real because it is internalised in the person's thinking. Right from the beginning various agents socialised him into accepting the world as they interpreted it. These agents were both the primary agents, such as one's parents, and other significant people who select certain aspects of the world to instill in us and who filter out others. There are also secondary agents such as the school and the media who may either confirm or disturb this interpretation given by the primary agents. This process of internalisation is not a superficial learning process but is so deep that it determines our view of things without our being aware that it is one of many possible interpretations. But, having said all this, we have so far failed to say something very important about man. Man is a creative being who not only receives society as given but creates society himself. He produces his own culture and world of meaning. There is then an ongoing dialectical process in which man is engaged between himself and society.

In short we might summarise the three phases involved in the making both of an individual and a society by saying that society emerges as a human product; that it takes upon itself the character of an objective reality and that when this happens it seems to act both upon man himself who thus becomes a socially produced being.

Religion, according to Berger, is constructed in exactly the same way as any other aspect of man's culture.[7] Language, mathematics, law or whatever are all human enterprises and social constructions. They help us to make sense of the world in which we live and to find meaning in a world that would otherwise be chaotic. What is different about religion is that its subject matter concerns the most ultimate questions. It explains why man is here; it deals with the threats which occur on the margins of man's existence such as dreams or death and it relates ordinary every day life to the most ultimate authority in the universe. It has to do with a sacred interpretation of life, that is, an interpretation that has a mysterious quality and awesome power about it.

This religious interpretation of the world is passed on from generation to generation and many will just accept and believe what they are told. But it is not and cannot be an unchanging phenomenon because man is not merely a passive receiver; he is also an active creator. In addition, the maintenance of any particular interpretation of reality by a believer depends on his having a structure which confirms his interpretation as plausible. This 'plausibility structure' is a social group who engage in conversation and practices which reinforce belief. They also offer explanations when our interpretation is threatened. And it stands to reason that, if we are to allow others to affirm our belief as true, these others must matter to us and be significant.

Two opposite threats are presented to a man's interpretation of the world and they have particular relevance for a religious world view. The belief held might be so commonly believed and accepted that it is not held with any degree of conviction or sense of reality but is just taken for granted. At the other end of the spectrum a person's belief may be threatened because his plausibility structure is reduced, weakened or disappears altogether.

Today's world is one where the latter has happened as far as the traditional Christian is concerned. Belief in God is no longer a socially given belief but has to be achieved by each private individual. Often when an individual does acquire faith in God, he finds only a very small plausibility structure to encourage him. What is more common today is that man is bombarded with a bewildering range of beliefs and options and, given the anti-dogmatic and tolerant age of which we are a part, it is very difficult to hold to any one particular position with integrity. The belief in a transcendent living God is made even more difficult because the prevailing atmosphere is one of rationalism, bureaucracy and the idea that eventually technology will be able to answer all man's problems.[8]

Berger has his own particular answers as to why it is possible to go on believing in God with integrity if the world really is as he describes.[9] The idea that *all* reality is socially constructed leaves open, he says, the question of whether or not a particular belief is true. He personally believes that the Judeo-Christian tradition corresponds most exactly to the reality which is there beyond man and of which man has to make sense. Further, he believes that looking objectively into human experience one can see pointers to this transcendent reality. He has recently written even more optimistically about the future survival of religion because he believes man will always need satisfying answers to the basic questions of whence, whither and why. The secular answers currently on offer, he claims are banal and can lead only to the 'pervasive boredom of a world without gods'.[10]

No one has yet applied Berger's views to the New Testament but the early Christian church would be a suitable subject to study both with a view to applying and testing the adequacy of his concepts. One can think immediately of a number of points that would require further investigation.

Firstly, we would need to see Jesus as a particularly creative individual. It is true that he stood to some extent in continuity with the religious interpretation of the world he received as a Jew. Yet he also stood in radical discontinuity from it. He spoke as a man with new insight and with a convincing authority which seemed to arise from personal knowledge as the gospels make clear. And he stood his ground with perfect consistency in the face of fierce opposition mounted by those who accepted the traditional religious interpretation of the world. What is more, he stood his ground when his own fragile plausibility structure, inhabited by his disciples and family, fell apart. He never seemed to be groping to explain reality; he always seemed to be in command as if reality was subject to him.

If there are some men who create reality rather than are shaped by it, Jesus must surely stand at the head of the list. But a reading of the gospels suggests that those who knew him would not have found it easy to fit him into Berger's normal categories of a man in a dialectical relationship with the world. John 1:1–18 would certainly place him outside of these normal categories.

Secondly, one wonders how easy it is to relate the idea of plausibility structures to the early Christians. Towards the end of the New Testament their importance becomes evident (e.g. Hebrews 10:25). But prior to that men came to believe in Jesus as the Messiah without reference to any particular structure and their belief often develops independently. It does not result from belonging to any particular plausibility structure. Paul is a classic case in point. He was well integrated into a

Jewish plausibility structure and yet independently of the Christians is converted. His early years as a Christian, as he himself emphasises, were ones where, despite some contact with the apostles, he was not too integrated into the rest of the church. Therefore, important as they are, plausibility structures cannot, be quite as determinative for belief as Berger seems to argue.

Thirdly, it is often assumed that interpreting the world in a religious way was easier in New Testament days than today, since a belief in the supernatural was more common and socially accepted and so those converted to Christianity would have little difficulty in making the switch from their previous faith. But, granting that there was a supernatural dimension in men's consciousness lacking in today's world, was it any easier for the early converts? Religious pluralism was as rife then as now. The Christian faith was certainly not a socially-given interpretation of the world. Men to a great extent were at home with other interpretations of the world and it would have been difficult to switch from one plausibility structure to another without personal cost. Those with 'homeless minds' may well have found a home in Christianity but, if so, we still have to ask why Christianity gave them the home for which they were looking.

This leads us fourthly to the question of the early Christian interpretation of the world. To Berger the language, concepts and interpretations we use are human productions which arise out of one's social situation and experience. They are the way we express what we have discovered in life. Clearly this partly accounts for the rich diversity to be found in the New Testament as Christians try to express what they discovered concerning Jesus. At times they have to admit that their discovery defies their ability to express it as in 2 Cor. 9:15.

Yet we are still left with the feeling that we have not quite fully grasped what the New Testament writers experienced. Their dominant confession was not of their human discoveries and their attempt to construct a religious universe of meaning. Their experience was of the inbreaking of the living God. He took the initiative; he was active in the first place and moved towards man. Rather than discovery their experience was of revelation. It was their united acclaim that Jesus was not merely a man who had discovered more about God than most men and having done so, passed the insights on. They claimed that he was God himself come to communicate with man; a visitor from beyond this world; the transcendent breaking in; God becoming fully a human being and revealing himself.

Sociologists understandably find it difficult to start their analysis with anything but man. Berger's search for a rumour of angels, that is, for some elementary evidence within man's own nature for the existence of a transcendent reality, however, shows how limited this approach must be. To have a certainty of God rather than merely a rumour of angels one has to start with God rather than man and with revelation rather than discovery. Sociology which begins and ends with man may then be poor sociology because it fails to take adequately into account man's repeated and real if somewhat elusive experience of a transcendent reality beyond and outside himself.

To argue in this way is not to say that belief places itself outside sociological analysis. It is to question the present narrow base of sociology and to ask that we continue to bear in mind one of the key aspects of Durkheim's approach to religion. One would dissent from Durkheim's conclusions that religion was a collective affair in which society worshipped itself or a symbol of itself and that by means of its collective effervescence it generated a great deal of spiritual cement which integrated individuals into the community. But Durkheim was surely right in his approach at least in this respect. Rejecting previous theories of religion which dismissed it as an illusion, hallucination or plain mistake, he argued that people who meet together to worship are worshipping something which is both real and beyond them.[11]

So, when the sociology of knowledge speaks of religion, as it does of everything else, as being socially constructed, we have to say that that does not quite get to the heart of the matter. If early Christianity was a religious interpretation which men themselves constructed, they were conscious of doing so because of an overwhelming reality which confronted them. Any construction in which they engaged was not their *creatio ex nihilo* but a simple expression of words which corresponded to a reality which already existed. To them it was not a social construction nor a human discovery. It was a belief based upon divine revelation—a revelation of God himself in human form in history. They believed as John said because, 'the Word became flesh and dwelt among us, full of grace and truth; we have beheld his glory, glory as of the only Son from the Father . . . No one has ever seen God; the only Son, who is in the bosom of the Father, he has made him known' (John 1:14, 18). Confronted with Jesus their lives were turned upside down; they stepped out of the normal socially-accepted paths of life and a powerful new community, called the Christian church, was founded.

Notes

CHAPTER ONE (pages 11–22)

1. E.g., Ernst Troeltsch, *The Social Teachings of the Christian Churches*, George Allen & Unwin, E.T. 1931, 1st German Ed., 1911. Shirley Jackson Case, *The Social Origins of Christianity*, University of Chicago Press, 1923. The greatest sociologist of religion, Max Weber, only mentions the New Testament Church in passing, *Ancient Judaism*, The Free Press, 1952, pp 421–424.
2. Howard Kee, *Community of the New Age*, S.C.M., 1977, p 9.
3. Peter L. Berger, *Invitation to Sociology*, Penguin Books, 1966, p 172.
4. For the best introduction to this field see Peter L. Berger and Thomas Luckmann, *The Social Construction of Reality*, Penguin Books, 1967. For its application to religion see Peter Berger, *The Social Reality of Religion*, Penguin Books, 1973.
5. Jonathan Z. Smith, 'The Social Description of Early Christianity', *Religious Studies Review*, i (1975), 19–21.
6. Clifford Hill, 'The Sociology of the New Testament', Unpublished Ph.D. Thesis, Nottingham, 1962, p 20.
7. ibid., p 15.
8. 2 Cor. 4:7.
9. Emile Durkheim, *The Elementary Forms of Religious Life*, George Allen and Unwin, 1976. (First Published in 1915).
10. 1 John 1:1–4; 3:19; 4:13 and 5:13.
11. An excellent article on these issues is to be found in *The Christian Graduate*, June, 1977, by J. A. Walter entitled, 'Sociology and Christianity, Some Conflicts and their Resolutions'.
12. Robin Gill, *The Social Context of Theology*, Mowbrays, 1975, deals in depth with this important issue.
13. Among a large range of literature one might mention, I. Howard Marshall (ed.), *New Testament Interpretation*, Paternoster Press, 1977. D. Guthrie, *New Testament Introduction*, I.V.P. 2nd Ed., 1970 and on an individual gospel a work such as I. Howard Marshall, *Luke: Historial and Theologian*, Paternoster Press, 1970.

14. op. cit., p 176.
15. Wayne A. Meeks, 'The Social World of Early Christianity', *Bulletin of the Council on the Study of Religion*, vi (1975), 1–5. A further recent survey can be found in R. Scroggs, 'The Sociological Interpretation of the New Testament: The Present state of research, *New Testament Studies*, xxvi (1980), 164–179.

CHAPTER TWO (pages 23–40)

1. E. A. Judge, *The Social Pattern of Christian Groups in the First Century*, Tyndale, 1960, p. 8f.
2. John A. Gager, *Kingdom and Community: The Social World of Early Christianity*, Prentice-Hall, 1975, p. 20.
3. Howard Kee, *Community of the New Age*, S.C.M., 1977, p. 176.
4. ibid., p. 107.
5. Kenelm Burridge, *New Heaven, New Earth*, Oxford, 1971, p. 3.
6. Bryan Wilson, *Magic and the Millennium*, Heinemann, 1973.
7. Yonina Talmon, 'The Pursuit of the Millennium: The Relation between Religious and Social Change', *Archives Europeannes de Sociologie*, iii, 1 (1962), 130.
8. For a popular exposition of the fully radical nature of the life and teaching of Jesus see Donald B. Kraybell, *The Upside-Down Kingdom*, Herald Press, 1978.
9. John A. Gager, op. cit., p. 24. For a more balanced discussion of Jesus' teaching on wealth see Dick France, 'Serving God or Mammon?', *Third Way*, ii, 10 (1978) 3–8.
10. ibid., p. 28.
11. Max Weber, *The Sociology of Religion*, Methuen & Co., 1965, Ch. 4.
12. J. Jeremias, *New Testament Theology*, Vol. 1., S.C.M., 1961, p. 66. Jeremias writes, 'We do not have a single example of God being addressed as 'Abba' in Judaism, but Jesus always addressed God in this way in his prayers.' For a discussion of this claim see J. D. G. Dunn, *Jesus and the Spirit*, S.C.M., 1975, pp. 21–26.
13. A full typology of 'responses to the world' is developed in Wilson, op. cit., pp. 19–30.
14. op. cit., p. 35.
15. Albert Schweitzer, *The Quest for the Historical Jesus*, 1906 (E. T., A. & C. Black, 1910).
16. For a summary of the developments see I. Howard Marshall, *I Believe in the Historical Jesus*, Hodder & Stoughton, 1977, ch. 6.
17. E. A. Judge, 'The Early Christians as a Scholastic Community', *Journal of Religious History*, i (1960–61), 4–15, 125–137.
18. ibid. p. 11.
19. ibid. p. 14f.

CHAPTER THREE (pages 41–50)

1. Gerd Theissen, *The First Followers of Jesus*, S.C.M., 1978 and 'Itinerant Radicalism: The Tradition of Jesus' sayings from the Perspective of the Sociology of Literature', *Radical Religion*, ii, 2 and 3, Berkeley (1975) 84–93. Much further background material is to be found in Joachim Jeremias, *Jerusalem in the time of Jesus*, S.C.M., 1967.
2. The Freudian perspective is heavily criticised by Bruce J. Malina, 'The Social Sciences and Biblical Interpretation', *Interpretation*, xxxvi (1982) 240.
3. See also Dick France, 'Serving God or Mammon?', *Third Way*, ii, 10 (1978) 3–8.
4. 'Itinerant Radicalism', p. 89.
5. *The First Followers*, p. 22.
6. David Mealand, *Poverty and Expectation in the Gospels*, S.P.C.K., 1980, p. 14.

CHAPTER FOUR (pages 51–64)

1. For a recent discussion regarding the historicity of *Acts* see M. Hengel, *Acts and the Historicity of Earliest Christianity*, S.C.M., 1979 and A. N. Sherwin-White, *Roman Society and Roman Law in the New Testament*, O.U.P., 1963.
2. Bryan Wilson (ed), *Patterns of Sectarianism*, Heinemann, 1967, Ch. 1 'An Analysis of Sect Development'.
3. Dean M. Kelly, *Why Conservative Churches are Growing*, Harper & Row, 1977. A thorough examination of the churches in the United States, by an ecumenical scholar, which distinguishes between strong and weak religious groups. Strong groups demand high commitment, exercise discipline and missionary zeal, hold absolute beliefs and are non-conformist as far as the world goes. Weak groups are the reverse. The strong groups, however, are the ones which are increasingly numerically.
4. J. M. Whitworth, *God's Blueprints*, Routledge & Kegan Paul, 1975. Foreword by David Martin, p. ix.
5. Ernst Haenchen, *The Acts of the Apostles*, Blackwell, 1971, p. 233.
6. Martin Hengel, *Property and Riches in the Early Church*, S.C.M., 1974, p. 34.
7. F. F. Bruce, 'The Early Church's Experiment in Communism', *Shaft*, No. 18, December, 1977, pp 6–8.
8. For a fuller discussion of this point see Derek J. Tidball, 'Perspectives on Community Living '*Vox Evangelica* XI (1979) pp 65–80.
9. Clifford Hill, 'The Sociology of the New Testament', Unpublished Ph.D., Nottingham, 1972, p. 48.
10. Max Weber, *The Theory of Social and Economic Organisation*,

The Free Press, 1964, Section III.
11. pp. 24ff.
12. Bengt Holmberg, *Paul and Power*, C. W. K. Gleerup, 1978, pp 72, 154.
13. ibid., pp 160f.
14. Hill, op. cit., 62f.
15. Joachim Jeremias, *Jerusalem in the Time of Jesus*, S.C.M., 1969, p. 232.
16. ibid., p. 266.
17. G. Kittel & G. Friedrich, eds., *Theological Dictionary of the New Testament*, Eerdmans, Vol. 4, p. 266. This interpretation assumes that the geographic references of Acts 6:9 explain who composes the Synagogue of the Freedmen. Acts 24:12 suggests that there may have been more than one synagogue; each of which would have been based on distinct national groups.
18. L. Festinger, H. Riecken and S. Schachter, *When Prophecy Fails*, Harper & Row, 1956.
    See also P. Henry, *New Directions in New Testament Study*, S.C.M., 1980, p. 187 f. This approach has also been applied to the Old Testament for which we see R. P. Carrol, *When Prophecy Fails*, S.C.M., 1979.
19. John G. Gager, *Kingdom and Community*, Prentice-Hall, 1975, pp 37–49.
20. F. F. Bruce, *The Acts of the Apostles*, Marshall, Morgan and Scott, 1954, p. 38.
21. For an excellent theological examination of the early Christians' motivation for mission see Michael Green, *Evangelism in the Early Church*, Hodder & Stoughton, 1970, ch. 9.

CHAPTER FIVE (pages 65–75)

1. For a fuller recent treatment of this subject see Eduard Lohse, *The New Testament Environment*, S.C.M., 1974.
2. M. Rostovtzeff, *The Social and Economic History of the Roman Empire*, Oxford, 2nd Ed. 1952, p. 29.
3. Vergil, *The Aeneid*, vi 791–2, cited in Hans Jurgen Schultz, *Jesus in His Time*, S.P.C.K., 1971, p. 3.
4. Rostovtzeff, op. cit., p. 84.
5. For a fuller account of the class system see John G. Gager, *Kingdom and Community*, Prentice-Hall, 1975, pp 96–106.
6. A. D. Nock, *Conversion*, The Old and the New in Religion from Alexander the Great to Augustine of Hippo, Oxford, 1933, p. 162.
7. Our society is not so much a secular society as a pluralistic one. See R. Towler, *Homo Religiosus*, Constable, 1974, pp 180–182 and Peter Berger, *Facing Up to Modernity*, Penguin, 1979, part 3.
8. See Michael Green, *Evangelism in the Early Church*, Hodder & Stoughton, 1970, ch. 9.

9. Colin Brown, (ed.), s.v. *'Lord'*, *New International Dictionary of New Testament Theology*, The Paternoster Press, Vol. 2, (1976) pp 508–520.
10. E. R. Dodds, *Pagan and Christian in an Age of Anxiety*, C.U.P., 1965, p. 133.
11. ibid, p. 135.

CHAPTER SIX (pages 76–89)

1. The basic analysis of this chapter is dependent on E. A. Judge, *The Social Pattern of Christian Groups in the First Century*, Tyndale Press, 1960.
2. ibid p. 20. Under Augustus nearly 100 states in Asia Minor issued their own currency and by the end of the 1st century this had risen to 300 states.
3. Robert Banks, *Paul's Idea of Community*, Paternoster Press, 1980, p. 20f.
4. In *A Home for the Homeless*, S.C.M., 1981, John Elliott has argued that in the case of 1 Peter at least three titles refer to the readers' social and political situation rather than their spiritual state. His supporting linguistic arguments are not wholly convincing. Since elsewhere it is plain that the word *parokoi* is used figuratively there seems no reason to differentiate its meaning in 1 Peter.
5. Floyd V. Filson, 'The Significance of the Early House Churches', *Journal of Biblical Literature*, 58, 1939, pp. 105–112.
6. Clifford Hill, 'The Sociology of the New Testament', Unpublished Ph.D., Thesis, Nottingham University, 1972, p. 215.
7. op. cit., p. 33f.
8. Emile Durkheim defined religion as 'a unified system of beliefs and practices relative to sacred things, i.e. things set apart and forbidden—beliefs and practices which unite into a single moral community called a church all those who adhere to them,' *Elementary Forms of Religious Life*, Allen & Unwin, First published 1915, 7th impression 1971, p. 47.
9. Banks, op. cit., p. 49 and 21, estimates that from the size of the large rooms in such houses the average Christian congregation was probably between 30 and 35, although the outside limits were probably 10 and 100.
10. The limitations to mission arise because (1) much energy, time, finance and personnel is invested in keeping a building in good repair; (2) public buildings are inflexible in their use and location; (3) they are impersonal especially when compared with homes and (4) they emphasise the need for people to come to a strange place in order to receive the gospel thus making an additional barrier between the hearer and the good news.
11. For detailed justification of this position see Banks, op. cit., pp. 41–48.

12. The whole matter of whether an individual in the New Testament world would perceive himself as an individual and the relationship he would feel to the corporate is explored in Bruce J. Malina, *The New Testament World*, S.C.M., 1983, pp. 51–70.
13. This issue receives further examination in George W. Peters, *Saturation Evangelism*, Zondervan, 1970, Part 3, pp. 145–222.
14. Filson does in fact mention this point but curiously only as a subsection of his point about the mixed social status of the early Christians.
15. A. D. Nock, *Conversion*, Oxford, 1933, p. 56f.
16. Cited in J. Stevenson (ed), *A New Eusebius*, S.P.C.K., 1968, p. 14. Other correspondence of Pliny shows that clubs had a bad reputation in this district. Trajan's ban therefore applied to that province and was not a general ban throughout the Empire.
17. C. Peter Wagner, 'Your Church can Grow', Regal, 1976, pp. 97–109 and Howard Snyder, New Wineskins, Marshall Morgan & Scott, 1977.

CHAPTER SEVEN (pages 90–103)

1. J. G. Gager, *Kingdom and Community*, Prentice-Hall, 1975, Ch. 4.
2. R. Niebuhr (ed.), F. Engels, 'On the History of Early Christianity', *Marx and Engels on Religion*, Schocken Press, 1964, p. 316 f.
3. Karl Kautsky, *Foundations of Christianity*, Orabis & Windrush, 1973 edition, pp. 9 and 323. The work was originally published in 1925.
4. ibid., p. 381.
5. Ernst Troeltsch, *The Social Teachings of the Christian Church*, Allen & Unwin, 1931, Vol. 1, p. 45f.
6. Adolf Deissmann, *Light from the Ancient East*, Hodder & Stoughton, 1927. See also the more recent discussion on the levels of literary culture in Abraham J. Malherbe, *Social Aspects of Early Christianity*, Lousiana State University Press, 1977, Ch. 2.
7. A sophist was a professional rhetorician who engaged in itinerant and scholarly debates and teaching. They grew in numbers in Paul's time and reached their peak in about the 2nd century AD. For a critical discussion of Paul as a sophist see Malherbe, pp. 45–59.
8. For an elaboration of the city of Tarsus see: F. F. Bruce, *Paul: Apostle of Free Spirit*, Paternoster Press, 1977, Chs. 3 and 4.
9. Clifford Hill, 'The Sociology of the New Testament', Unpublished Ph.D. Thesis, University of Nottingham, 1972, p. 201. This could be explained in terms of Paul's view of apostolic authority, which Hill neglects. Nevertheless the point Hill makes is well taken.
10. The leading men are not mentioned at Lystra but presumably, since they made no attempt to restrain the violence, they knew of it and endorsed it.
11. E. A. Judge, 'Early Christians as a Scholastic Community', *Journal*

of Religious History, Vol. 1, 1960–61, p. 127. In this article Judge tries to compare Paul with other contemporary sophists. Although the detailed research is helpful the attempt to present the early Christians as a scholastic community is not altogether convincing.

12. Shirley Jackson Case, *The Social Origins of Christianity*, University of Chicago Press, 1923, pp. 167–170.
13. For a recent discussion of the problem see C. E. B. Canfield, *Romans*, International Critical Commentary, T. and T. Clark, 1975, Vol. 1, pp. 5–11.
14. Anthony C. Thiselton, 'Realised Eschatology at Corinth', *New Testament Studies*, 24, 1978, pp. 510–526.
15. Gerd Theissen finds four criteria necessary for establishing who the people of high social status were: (1) civil or religious office in the city of Corinth, (2) to possess a 'house', (3) to have been of material service to Paul or the church and (4) having the ability to make journeys. The last two criteria do not stand on their own. *The Social Setting of Pauline Ministry*, T. and T. Clark, 1982, pp. 73–96.
16. op. cit., p. 130.
17. 'Paul does not deny the continuing legitimacy of national, social and sexual differences—Paul is no advocate of a universal, classless and unisex society—he merely affirms that these differences do not affect one's relationship with Christ and membership in the community. There is an egalitarian strain in Paul's pronouncement but it is secondary.' Robert Banks, *Paul's Idea of Community*, Paternoster Press, 1980, p. 118.
18. Theissen, op. cit., pp. 145–174.
19. e.g. W. Hollenweger, *The Pentecostals*, S.C.M., 1972, pp. 459–467.
20. op. cit., p. 188f.
21. e.g. Virginia Hine, 'The Deprivation and Disorganisation Theories of Social Movements', Irving I. Zaretsky and Mark P. Leone (eds.), *Religious Movements in Contemporary America*, Princeton University Press, 1974, pp. 646–661.

CHAPTER EIGHT (pages 104–122)

1. One assumes that in spite of the difficulties which remain with the work Max Weber has established beyond serious doubt the influence ideas can have on behaviour. See *The Protestant Ethic and the Spirit of Capitalism*, Unwin University Books, 1930.
2. J. L. Houlden, *Ethics and the New Testament*, Penguin Books, 1973, p. 23, argues that Paul is here using a list of conventional ethics.
3. ibid., pp. 66–69.
4. ibid., pp. 25–34.
5. H. Ridderbos, *Paul, An Outline of his Theology*, Eerdmans, 1975,

pp. 487–497 and D. Guthrie, *New Testament Theology*, IVP, 1981, pp. 809 f.

6. For a lengthy elaboration of the sectarian nature of the early church in relation to the social status of its members and the effect of external opposition, see John H. Elliott, *A Home for the Homeless*, S.C.M., 1982.

7. Bryan Wilson, *Magic and the Millenium*, Heinmann, 1973, pp. 31–69. Wilson uses 'utopian' in a different way to that of David Martin referred to earlier.

8. Jack. T. Sanders, *Ethics in the New Testament*, Fortress Press, 1975. Sanders explains the point in these words, 'Since it is now the time of the dawn of the day of God's righteousness, the long awaited day, the day in which one *will* be able to fulfill the law, to love, to do the good *without* the limitation of the ei dynaton, for that reason it is time to 'put off the works of darkness' and 'to clothe oneself with the weapons of light'—that is, the imminence of the eschaton makes the imperative possible.' p. 61.

9. For a more balanced discussion of the relationship between Revelation and other parts of the New Testament, see G. R. Beasley-Murray, *The Book of Revelation*, Oliphants, 1974, pp. 38–48.

10. op. cit., p. 114.

11. John G. Gager, *Kingdom and Community*, Prentice-Hall, 1975, pp. 49–57. The victory/hope cycle is 4:1–5:14; 7:1–8:4; 10:1–11:1; 11:15–19; 14:1–7; 15:2–8; 19:1–16 and 21:1–22:5. The oppression/despair cycle is 6:1–7; 8:5–9:21; 11:2–14; 12:1–17; 13:1–18; 14:8–15:2; 16:2–20; 17:1–18:24 and 19:17–20:15.

12. John R. W. Stott, *God's New Society*, I.V.P., 1979, p. 9. An exposition of Ephesians which has as its main theme the nature of the new society which had been formed by Christ.

13. The doctrines and principles were numerous and well-defined and this view does not lead to situation ethics as commonly understood; on which see David Field, *Free to do Right*, I.V.P., 1973, pp. 24–38.

14. Oscar Cullmann, *The State in the New Testament*, S.C.M., 1957, p. 56.

15. ibid., p. 57.

16. Ridderbos, op. cit., pp. 320–326.

17. op. cit., p. 83.

18. William Westermann, *The Slave Systems of Greek and Roman Antiquity*, The American Philosophical Society, 1955, Vol. 40, p. 117.

19. J. Carcopino, *Daily Life in Ancient Rome*, Penguin, 1964, p. 69f.

20. R. H. Barrow, *The Romans*, Penguin Books, 1949, p. 99f.

21. Westermann, op. cit., p. 150, and pp. 152–156 for details of the debate.

22. ibid., pp. 152–156.

23. David Mealand, *Poverty and Expectation in the Gospels*, S.P.C.K., 1980, p. 38ff.

24. ibid., pp. 73, 83, and 87.

25. ibid., p. 93. See also, M. Hengel, *Property and Riches in the Early*

Church, S.C.M., 1973, ch. 12, 'Ten Concluding Theses'.
26. Ernst Troeltsch, *The Social Teachings of the Christian Churches*, Allen & Unwin, 1931, Vol. 1, pp. 82–86.
27. ibid., p. 80.
28. ibid., p. 85.
29. J. D. Douglas (ed.), *Let the Earth Hear His Voice*, World Wide Publications, 1975, pp. 3–9, clauses 10 and 5 respectively.

CHAPTER NINE (pages 123–136)

1. D. O. Moberg, *The Church as a Social Institution*, Prentice-Hall, 1962 pp. 118–124.
2. Eddie Gibbs, *Body-building Exercises for the Local Church*, Falcon, 1979, p. 24.
3. This definition is based on Moberg's definition, op. cit., p. 22 '... the process by which social functions, relationships and values gradually or suddenly become crystallised, formalised or stabilised so that they produce a relatively uniform behaviour among groups and organisational groupings.'
4. The words 'sect' and 'denomination' here are being used technicaly in the sociological sense for a discussion of which see Michael Hill, *A Sociology of Religion*, Heinemann, 1973, chs 3 and 4 or R. Robertson, *The Sociological Interpretaion of Religion*, Blackwell, 1970, ch 5.
5. T. F. O'Dea, 'Five Dilemmas in the Institutionalisation of Religion', *Sociology and the Study of Religion*, Basic Books, 1970, pp. 241–254. For a briefer version see T. F. O'Dea, *The Sociology of Religion*, Prentice-Hall, 1966, pp. 90–97.
6. ibid, p. 279.
7. Ernst Troeltsch, *The Social Teachings of the Christian Church*, Allen & Unwin, Vol. 1, 1931, p. 62.
8. For a discussion of their authenticity see D. Guthrie, *New Testament Introduction*, IVP, 1970, R. Martin, *New Testament Foundations*, Paternoster Press, 1978, Vol. 2.
9. J. D. G. Dunn, *Unity and Diversity in the New Testament*, S.C.M., 1977, p. 351. Dunn has a section, pp. 351–359 on 'Increasing Institutionalisation'. He wisely rejects the idea that the high view of the church in Ephesians is evidence of institutionalization since in so many other ways Paul's view of the church here corresponds to that elsewhere in his writings.
10. For a discussion of these issues in depth see D. Guthrie, *The Pastoral Epistles*, Tyndale Press, 1957, pp. 24–32,: J. N. D. Kelly, *The Pastoral Epistles*, A. and C. Black, 1963, pp. 13–16 and Dunn, ibid, p. 352.
11. ibid, pp. 114–116.
12. Guthrie, op. cit., p. 42f.
13. For a critical review of Dunn's work which argues that orthodoxy was not a late invention see R. T. France, *Themelios*, 5, 1979. p. 30f.
14. Kelly, op. cit., p. 17.

CHAPTER TEN (pages 137–142)

1. For the literature of these and other points, see J. A. Gager, *Kingdom and Community*, Prentice-Hall, 1975, Chs. 3 and 5.

2. To use sociological tools to futher the mission of the church is not generally referred to as the sociology of religion so much as religious sociology. Religious sociology owes much to the French Catholic scholar Ferdinand Boulard. For an English example, see M. J. Jackson, *The Sociology of Religion*, Batsford, 1974. For a critique which argues for the abandonment of the distinction see Robin Gill, *The Social Context of Theology*, Mowbrays, 1975, ch. 2.

3. The church growth movement explicitly applies sociological analysis to the church with the aim of using the results to aid the church's growth. Though a diffuse movement it is largely evangelical and one of its chief centres is the school of World Mission at Fuller Theological Seminary, Pasadena, California. As an evangelical movement it seeks to justify its findings not only by reference to contemporary sociology but also by reference to the practice of the early church as recorded in Scripture. Representative works where this combined approach is seen are: Donald McGavran, *Understanding Church Growth*, Eerdmans, 1970; C. Peter Wagner, *Your Church Can Grow*, Regal, 1976; and Alan Tippet, *Church Growth and the Word of God*, Eerdmans, 1970; and E. Gibbs, *I Believe in Church Growth*, Hodder & Stoughton, 1981.

4. Eileen Stevenson, 'Some Insights from the Sociology of Religion into the Origin and Development of the early Christian Church', *Expository Times* XC (1979), 300–305.

5. Robin Scroggs, 'The Sociological Interpretation of the New Testament: The Present State of Research', *New Testament Studies*, 26 (1980). 164–179.

6. P. Berger and T. Luckmann, *The Social Construction of Reality*, Penguin, 1967.

7. P. Berger, *The Social Reality of Religion*, Penguin, 1973.

8. P. Berger, B. Berger and H. Kellner, *The Homeless Mind*, Penguin, 1974.

9. P. Berger, *A Rumour of Angels*, Penguin, 1970.

10. P. Berger, *Facing up to Modernity*, Penguin, 1979, ch. 13.

11. E. Durkheim, *The Elementary Forms of Religious Life*, Allen & Unwin, first published 1915, 7th impression, chs. 2 and 3.

Bibliography

R. Banks, *Paul's Idea of Community*, Paternoster Press, 1980.
R. H. Barrow, *The Romans*, Penguin Books, 1949.
G. R. Beasley-Murray, *The Book of Revelation*, Oliphants, 1974.
P. L. Berger, *A Rumour of Angels*, Penguin, 1970.
P. L. Berger, *Facing up to Modernity*, Penguin, 1979.
P. L. Berger, B. Berger and H. Kellner, *The Homeless Mind*, Penguin, 1974.
P. L. Berger, *Invitation to Sociology*, Penguin, 1966.
P. L. Berger, *The Social Reality of Religion*, Penguin, 1973.
P. L. Berger and T. Luckmann, *The Social Construction of Reality*, Penguin, 1967.
C. Brown (ed), *Dictionary of New Testament Theology*, i–iii, Paternoster Press, 1975, 1976, 1978.
F. F. Bruce, *The Acts of the Apostles*, Marshall, Morgan & Scott, 1954.
F. F. Bruce, 'The Early Church's Experiment in Communism', *Shaft* 18, (1977) 6–8.
F. F. Bruce, *Paul: Apostle of the Free Spirit*, Paternoster Press, 1977.
K. Burridge, *New Heaven, New Earth*, Oxford University Press, 1971.
J. Carcopino, *Daily Life in Ancient Rome*, Penguin, 1964.
R. P. Carrol, *When Prophecy Failed*, S.C.M., 1979.
S. J. Case, *The Social Origins of Christianity*, University of Chicago Press, 1923.
C. E. B. Cranfield, *Romans*, i–ii, ICC, T. and T. Clark, 1975, 1979.
O. Cullmann, *The State in the New Testament*, S.C.M., 1957.
A. Deissmann, *Light from the Ancient East*, Hodder & Stoughton, 1927.
E. R. Dodds, *Pagan and Christian in an Age of Anxiety*, Cambridge University Press, 1965.
J. D. Douglas (ed), *Let the Earth Hear His Voice*, World Wide Publications, 1975.
J. D. G. Dunn, *Jesus and the Spirit*, S.C.M., 1975.

J. D. G. Dunn, *Unity and Diversity in the New Testament*, S.C.M., 1977.

E. Durkheim, *The Elementary Forms of Religious Life*, George Allen & Unwin, 1976 (first edition, 1915).

J. Elliott, *A Home for the Homeless*, A Sociological Exegesis of 1 Peter, S.C.M., 1981.

L. Festinger, H. Riecken and S. Schachter, *When Prophecy Fails*, Harper & Row, 1956.

D. Field, *Free to do Right*, IVP., 1973.

F. V. Filson, 'The Significance of the Early House Churches', *Journal of Biblical Literature*, 58 (1939) 105–112.

R. T. France, 'Serving God or Mammon?', *Third Way*, ii, 10 (1978) 3–8.

J. A. Gager, *Kingdom and Community: The Social World of Early Christianity*, Prentice-Hall, 1975.

J. G. Gager, 'Shall We Marry Our Enemies?' *Interpretation*, xxxvi (1982) 256–265.

E. Gibbs, *Body-Building Exercises for the Local Church*, Falcon Press, 1979.

E. Gibbs, *I Believe in Church Growth*, Hodder & Stoughton, 1981.

R. Gill, *The Social Context of Theology*, Mowbrays, 1975.

M. Green, *Evangelism in the Early Church*, Hodder & Stoughton, 1970.

D. Guthrie, *New Testament Introduction*, IVP, 1970 (second edition).

D. Guthrie, *New Testament Theology*, IVP., 1981.

D. Guthrie, *The Pastoral Epistles*, Tyndale Press, 1957.

E. Haenchen, *The Acts of the Apostles*, Blackwells, 1971.

M. Hengel, *Property and Riches in the Early Church*, S.C.M., 1974.

P. Henry, *New Directions in New Testament Study*, S.C.M., 1980.

C. Hill, 'The Sociology of the New Testament', Unpublished Ph.D., Thesis, Nottingham University, 1962.

M. Hill, *A Sociology of Religion*, Heinemann, 1973.

V. Hine, 'The Deprivation and Disorganisation Theories of Social Movements', *Religious Movements in Contemporary America*, I. I. Zaretsky and M. P. Leone (eds), Princeton University Press, 1974.

W. Hollenweger, *The Pentecostals*, S.C.M., 1972.

B. Holmberg, *Paul and Power*, C. W. K. Gleerup, 1978.

J. L. Houlden, *Ethics and the New Testament*, Penguin, 1973.

M. J. Jackson, *The Sociology of Religion*, Batsford, 1974.

J. Jeremias, *Jerusalem in the Time of Jesus*, S.C.M., 1969.

J. Jeremias, *New Testament Theology*, i, S.C.M., 1961.

E. A. Judge, 'The Early Christians as a Scholastic Community', *Journal of Religious History*, i (1960–61) 4–15, 125–137.

E. A. Judge, *The Social Pattern of Christian Groups in the First Century*, Tyndale Press, 1960.

K. Kautsky, *Foundations of Christianity*, Orabis & Windrush, 1973.

H. Kee, *Christian Origins in Sociological Perspective*, S.C.M., 1980.

H. Kee, *Community of the New Age*, S.C.M., 1977.

D. M. Kelly, *Why Conservative Churches are Growing*, Harper & Row, 1977.

J. N. D. Kelly, *The Pastoral Epistles*, A. and C. Black, 1963.

G. Kittel and G. Friedrich (eds), *Theological Dictionary of the New Testament*, Eerdmans, 1964–1976.

D. B. Kraybill, *The Upside-Down Kingdom*, Herald Press, 1978.

E. Lohse, *The New Testament Environment*, S.C.M., 1974.

A. J. Malherbe, *Social Aspects of Early Christianity*, Louisiana State University Press, 1977.

B. J. Malina, *The New Testament World*, Insights from Cultural Anthropology, S.C.M., 1983.

B. J. Malina, 'The Social Sciences and Biblical Interpretation', *Interpretation*, xxxvi (1982) 229–242.

I. H. Marshall, *I Believe in the Historical Jesus*, Hodder & Stoughton, 1972.

I. H. Marshall, *Luke: Historian and Theologian*, Paternoster Press, 1970, 1978.

I. H. Marshall (ed), *New Testament Interpretation*, Paternoster Press, 1977.

R. Martin, *New Testament Foundations*, i–ii, Paternoster Press, 1975, 1978.

D. McGavran, *Understanding Church Growth*, Eerdmans, 1970.

D. Mealand, *Poverty and Expectation in the Gospels*, S.P.C.K., 1980.

W. A. Meeks, 'The Social World of Early Christianity', *Bulletin of the Council on the Study of Religion*, vi (1975) 1–5.

D. O. Moberg, *The Church as a Social Institution*, Prentice-Hall, 1962.

R. Niebuhr (ed), *Marx and Engels on Religion*, Schocken Press, 1964.

A. D. Nock, *Conversion*. The Old and New in Religion from Alexander the Great to Augustine of Hippo, Oxford University Press, 1933.

T. F. O'Dea, *The Sociology of Religion*, Prentice-Hall, 1966.

T. F. O'Dea, *Sociology and the Study of Religion*, Basic Books, 1970.

G. W. Peters, *Saturation Evangelism*, Zondervan, 1970.

H. Ridderbos, *Paul*. An outline of his Theology, Eerdmans, 1975.

R. Robertson, *The Sociological Interpretation of Religion*, Blackwell, 1970.

M. Rostovtzeff, *The Social and Economic History of the Roman Empire*, Oxford University Press, 1952 (second edition).

J. T. Sanders, *Ethics in the New Testament*, Fortress Press, 1975.

J. H. Schultz, *Jesus in His Time*, S.P.C.K., 1971.

A. Schweitzer, *The Quest for the Historical Jesus*, A. and C. Black, (ET) 1910.

R. Scroggs, 'The Sociological Interpretation of the New Testament: The Present State of Research', *New Testament Studies*, xxvi (1980) 164–179.

J. Z. Smith, 'The Social Description of Early Christianity', *Religious*

Studies Review, i (1975) 19–21.

H. Snyder, *New Wineskins*, Marshall, Morgan & Scott, 1977.

E. Stevenson, 'Some Insights from the Sociology of Religion into the Origin and Development of the Early Christian Church', *Expository Times*, xc (1979) 300–305.

J. Stevenson (ed), *A New Eusebius*, S.P.C.K., 1968.

J. R. W. Stott, *God's New Society*, IVP., 1979.

Y. Talmon, 'The Pursuit of the Millenium: The Relation between Religions and Social Change', *Archives Européennes de Sociologie*, iii (1962), 125–148.

G. Theissen, *The First Followers of Jesus*, S.C.M., 1978.

G. Theissen, 'Itinerant Radicalism: The Tradition of Jesus's Sayings from the Perspective of the Sociology of Literature', *Radical Religion*, ii (1975) 84–93.

G. Theissen, *The Social Setting of Pauline Christianity*, T. and T. Clark 1982.

A. C. Thiselton, 'Realised Eschatology at Corinth', *New Testament Studies*, xxiv (1978) 510–526.

D. J. Tidball, 'Perspectives of Community Living', *Vox Evangelica*, xi (1979), 65–80.

A. Tippet, *Church Growth and the Word of God*, Eerdmans, 1970.

R. Towler, *Homo Religiosus*, Constable, 1974.

E. Troeltsch, *The Social Teaching of the Christian Churches*, George Allen and Unwin (ET) 1931, (First published 1911).

C. P. Wagner, *Your Church Can Grow*, Regal, 1976.

J. A. Walter, 'Sociology and Christianity. Some Conflicts and their Resolutions', *Christian Graduate*, June 1977, 37–46.

M. Weber, *Ancient Judaism*, The Free Press, 1952.

M. Weber, *The Protestant Ethic and the Spirit of Capitalism*, Unwin University Books, 1930.

M. Weber, *The Sociology of Religion*, Methuen, 1965 (first edition, 1922).

M. Weber, *The Theory of Social and Economic Organisation*, The Free Press, 1964 (first edition, 1947).

W. Westermann, *The Slave Systems of Greek and Roman Antiquity*, The American Philosophical Society, xc 1955.

J. M. Whitworth, *God's Blueprints*, Routledge & Kegan Paul, 1975.

B. Wilson, *Magic and the Millenium*, Heinemann, 1973.

B. Wilson (ed.), *Patterns of Sectarianism*. Heinemann, 1967.

Index of Biblical Passages

Index of Modern Authors